activating
the heart

Indigenous Studies Series

The Indigenous Studies Series builds on the successes of the past and is inspired by recent critical conversations about Indigenous epistemological frameworks. Recognizing the need to encourage burgeoning scholarship, the series welcomes manuscripts drawing upon Indigenous intellectual traditions and philosophies, particularly in discussions situated within the Humanities.

activating
the heart

STORYTELLING
KNOWLEDGE SHARING
AND RELATIONSHIP

JULIA CHRISTENSEN, CHRISTOPHER COX,
AND LISA SZABO-JONES, EDITORS

WILFRID LAURIER
UNIVERSITY PRESS

LAURIER
Inspiring Lives.

Wilfrid Laurier University Press acknowledges the support of the Canada Council for the Arts for our publishing program. We acknowledge the financial support of the Government of Canada through the Canada Book Fund for our publishing activities. This work was supported by the Research Support Fund.

Library and Archives Canada Cataloguing in Publication

Activating the heart : storytelling, knowledge sharing, and relationship / Julia Christensen, Christopher Cox, and Lisa Szabo-Jones, editors.

(Indigenous studies series)
Includes bibliographical references and index.
Issued in print and electronic formats.
ISBN 978-1-77112-219-1 (softcover).—ISBN 978-1-77112-220-7 (PDF).—
ISBN 978-1-77112-221-4 (EPUB)

1. Storytelling—Social aspects—Canada. 2. Discourse analysis, Narrative—Social aspects—Canada. 3. Indians of North America—Canada. I. Christensen, Julia, [date], editor II. Cox, Christopher, [date], editor III. Szabo-Jones, Lisa, [date], editor IV. Series: Indigenous studies series

P302.7.A28 2018   808.5'43   C2017-902753-0
                                                              C2017-902754-9

Cover photo by Lisa Szabo-Jones.
Cover and text design by Sandra Friesen.

"sleepless in Somba K'e," by Rita Wong, from *undercurrent* (Nightwood Editions, 2015), is reproduced with permission of Nightwood Editions.

This book is printed on FSC® certified paper and is certified Ecologo. It contains post-consumer fibre, is processed chlorine free, and is manufactured using biogas energy.

Printed in Canada

Every reasonable effort has been made to acquire permission for copyright material used in this text, and to acknowledge all such indebtedness accurately. Any errors and omissions called to the publisher's attention will be corrected in future printings.

RECYCLED
Paper made from
recycled material
FSC® C103567

Contents

LIST OF ILLUSTRATIONS   vii

ACKNOWLEDGEMENTS   ix

INTRODUCTION
Julia Christensen, Christopher Cox, and Lisa Szabo-Jones   xi

Section One   Storytelling to Understand

CHAPTER ONE
Finding My Way: Emotions and Ethics in Community-Based Action
Research with Indigenous Communities
Leonie Sandercock   3

CHAPTER TWO
Notes from the UNDERBRIDGE
Christine Stewart and Jacquie Leggatt   29

CHAPTER THREE
Re-valuing Code-Switching: Lessons from Kaska Narrative Performances
Patrick Moore   53

Section Two   Storytelling to Share

CHAPTER FOUR
Art, Heart, and Health: Experiences from Northern British Columbia
Kendra Mitchell-Foster and Sarah de Leeuw   91

CHAPTER FIVE
"Grandson, / This is meat": Hunting Metonymy in François Mandeville's
This Is What They Say
Jasmine Spencer   119

Section Three   Storytelling to Create

CHAPTER SIX
sleepless in Somba K'e
Rita Wong   145

CHAPTER SEVEN
Old Rawhide Died
Bren Kolson   147

CHAPTER EIGHT
Métis Storytelling across Time and Space: Situating the Personal and
Academic Self Between Homelands
Zoe Todd   153

CONCLUSION
Julia Christensen, Christopher Cox, and Lisa Szabo-Jones   171

REFERENCES   181
ABOUT THE CONTRIBUTORS   199
INDEX   203

List of Illustrations

FIGURE 2.1 "Listen"   29

FIGURE 3.1 Map of Kaska traditional territory   54

FIGURE 3.2 John Dickson, circa 1925   57

FIGURE 3.3 Maudie Dick, Ross River, Yukon, 1986   68

FIGURE 3.4 John Dickson, Frances Lake, Yukon, 1992   72

FIGURE 4.1 The Nak'azdli Health Centre, Nak'azdli First Nation   95

FIGURE 4.2 Kwah Hall at Nak'azdli First Nation, during ArtDays   96

FIGURE 4.3 The University of Northern British Columbia campus
            in Prince George, where the Northern Medical Program
            is located   97

FIGURE 4.4 A day picking berries in the northern hot summer sun   101

FIGURE 4.5 Artmaking at Stuart Lake   102

FIGURE 4.6 Art created by people participating in Nak'azdli Art Days   106

FIGURE 4.7 Art produced by Indigenous youth participants in the
            T-shirt workshop, depicting positive imagery   114

FIGURE 5.1 Untitled   126

FIGURE 5.2 Untitled   137

Acknowledgements

This modest book emerges from many generous collaborations, from inception of the Activating the Heart Yellowknife workshop to this collection's completion. Neither would have been possible without funding from the Government of the Northwest Territories Department of Health and Social Services, the Northwest Territories Arts Council, the Social Sciences and Humanities Research Council of Canada, the Institute for Circumpolar Health Research, the Pierre Elliott Trudeau Foundation, the Prince of Wales Northern Heritage Centre, Maria Campbell, Warren Cariou, and Jeremy Webber. Maria, Warren, Jeremy, and Val Napoleon were instrumental in providing institutional and financial support and counsel: Thank you.

This collection started as a cross-cultural and cross-disciplinary conversation over three days. A heartfelt thank-you to Yellowknives Dene (Weledeh) community for generously hosting us at the Chief Drygeese Centre in Dettah, as well as to Elders Alfred Baillargeon, Fred Sangris, and Modeste and Therese Sangris for guiding the direction of this conversation. A special thank you to Mary Rose Sundberg for her mentorship and support, as well as to Lina Drygeese, Jeanie Martin, and other Goyatiko Language Society interpreters for their thoughtful work in ensuring meaningful exchange over the course of the workshop. We would also like to thank Bobby and Jennifer Drygeese for hosting our group at the B Dene Cultural Camp. Mahsi cho.

Andrée Boisselle was a key collaborator of ours in organizing the initial workshop; merci beaucoup for your contributions and generous spirit. Our everlasting appreciation also to the workshop participants for your engagement and encouragement. Workshop participants who do not appear in this volume, but whose thoughtful dialogue helped to form the foundation for this collection's chapters, include Cindy Allen, Paul Andrew, Marie-Claire Belleau, Diane Conrad, Clayton Episkenew, Jo-Ann Episkinew, Margery Fee, Stephanie Irlbacher-Fox, Sarah Jerome, Rebecca Johnson, Darcy Leigh, Nehraz Mahmud, Keavy Martin, Lyana Patrick, Leila Qashu, Deanna Reder, Olivia Sammons, Carla Suarez, Anne Thrasher, Richard Van Camp, Katrin Wittig, and Edmonton's iHuman Youth Society Project members Melissa Bigstone, Tabitha Blair, Cory Nicotine, Brianna Olson, Stephanie Palmer, and Nicole Webb. Our gratitude also to Jill Christensen and family for nourishing us with delicious food and hospitality. Hai hai. Qujannamiik. Tak. Merci. Thank you. Miigwech.

Thank you to all the contributors and to Wilfrid Laurier University Press and the Indigenous Studies Series advisory board for helping us see this collection to its publication. A special thank-you to Lisa Quinn, Siobhan McMenemy, the reviewers, Rob Kohlmeier, and the copy editors.

Introduction

Julia Christensen, Christopher Cox,
and Lisa Szabo-Jones

The sharing of knowledge across languages and epistemologies is never a matter of simply exchanging one word for another; it is finding a way to convey
accurately the deepest levels of meaning from one cultural milieu or knowledge tradition to another. Attempts to relate to communities, and particularly
to Indigenous communities, too often fall short because academic research
remains largely rooted in colonial ways of seeing and knowing (for example,
privileging research methods and forms of communication geared towards
acquiring information to provide concrete outcomes rather than those
aimed at entering open-ended, long-term relationships). Such institutional
languages and learning modes often conflict with the ways in which many
academics actually engage with their research. Given the dominance of these
languages, scholars seeking to develop their skills and to gain proficiency in
alternative modes of engagement face many hurdles. The result is a radical
impoverishment of our social, political, and environmental imagination. In
this respect, *Activating the Heart* is timely, in that the collection seeks to make
room for a different kind of education, one that builds necessary ties between
community and academia to engender a space for broader, non-oppressive
education models. Doing so requires not only bridging academic and community contexts but also embracing different ways of storytelling, from the
spiritual and the emotional to the artistic and the creative, to engage diverse
audiences and inspire change. Thus, this collection speaks to academics;
however, because of the contributors' broad artistic, historic, and cultural
range, *Activating the Heart* will appeal also to non-academics.

Activating the Heart is the collaborative outcome of engaging academics with the teachings of community-based knowledges. Over a warm, sunny June week in Yellowknife, Northwest Territories, a group of storytellers, researcher-storytellers, and Elders gathered at the Chief Drygeese Centre on Yellowknives Dene First Nation territory for a workshop titled Activating the Heart: Storytelling, Knowledge Sharing and Relationship, intended specifically to address cross-cultural engagement and responsibility. The workshop participants were all people who bridge multiple contexts in their work—academic, community, spiritual, creative—to engage diverse audiences and inspire change in meaningful ways. Over the course of three days, participants shared stories, research projects, and experiences with one another and collectively explored the role of storytelling in sharing knowledge and building understanding across different cultures and contexts. Through discussion, we explored storytelling as a means not only to illustrate research themes but also to communicate ideas in a more immediate and engaging way. For many participants, the cross-cultural exchange put into new perspective both our purpose as researchers and storytellers and the importance of trust-building between research creation making and community. We left with a deeper appreciation for the power of story in our work and the ways in which storytelling presents opportunities for a "reorienting" of the research process and form and of its content.

In this collection, authors examine storytelling as a mode of understanding, sharing, and creating knowledge. Storytelling is more than just a methodology—it is a mode of knowledge production and dissemination, which takes multiple creative or artistic forms. What is *research* storytelling, though? We, the editors, by way of example, come from different disciplines: geography, linguistics, and literary criticism. In the social sciences, research storytelling, also known as narrative research, incorporates the stories of the participants or researchers as part of the qualitative analysis. How a story is told and by whom, a reflexive turn to the research process, has significant influence on how problems are approached. In the arts and humanities, research storytelling often falls under arts-based research or creative research making. The researcher incorporates regular artistic practices into the scholarly qualitative inquiry "as a primary way of understanding and examining experiences" (McNiff 2008, 29). Regardless of title, and as the contributions of this collection attest, research storytelling emphasises creative intelligence as the heart of knowledge communication, acquisition, and retention. Synthesizing storytelling and research commits to the belief that narrative will direct listeners to transformative connections, that "[i]n keeping with the dynamics of creative process, what appears most removed from the problem at hand may offer a useful way of transforming it" (McNiff 2008, 32). This opens a question: If research's mandate is to produce and share knowledge in meaningful ways, then why is story or artistic representation rarely a component of published scholarly discourse?

Perhaps there is resistance because storytelling implicates personal introspection that contradicts the objectivity of scholarly pursuit. This debate is not new, nor is it dead. Stories saturate our daily lives. Storytelling requires listening. Storytelling, an artistic investigation, becomes, to borrow McNiff's words, the "creation of a process of inquiry" (2008, 33). McNiff contends that art invites us to start with questions to discover a method of approach to suit the situation, rather than, as most academic disciplines do, fitting the questions into the methodology (2008, 33). Expanding upon his point, we hold that storytelling's emphasis on listening creates a reflective, responsive space that opens the problem to dialogue and to processual and adaptive thinking. In this way, *Activating the Heart* pays specific attention to the significance of storytelling in Indigenous knowledge frameworks, while also extending into other ways of knowing in which scholars have embraced narrative and story as a part of their research approach.

While education is one area in which communication of research is fostered, Eurocentric education models, as Marie Battiste claims, have neglected to "enrich the future of other peoples" through Indigenous people's "inherent capacity to foster participatory consciousness with our environment, ecology, and the inner spirits" (2014, 91). Battiste's point is clear: educational reform—the decolonization of Eurocentric scholarship models—must be transformative in ways that connect relationships of inequity to and beyond academic institutions. For changes to occur, alliances are needed that "[continue] to contest the layers of contradictions and paradoxes in discourses, histories, assumptions, beliefs, and values between Indigenous and non-Indigenous peoples" (Battiste 2014, 91). Together, the chapters in this collection foster an interdisciplinary and cross-cultural dialogue that offers a small, but significant, contribution to this ongoing work: qualitative research methods, policy-making, activism, artistic practice, meaning, and healing.

The overall question framing *Activating the Heart* considers how storytelling advances responsibility and relationship at the local, national, and global levels. To create a space for meaningful exchange between people of various creative traditions and backgrounds, we collectively embrace and explore the diverse ways in which storytelling as knowledge production and sharing builds new interconnections between people, their histories, their environments, and their cultural geographies and contributes to relationship. Thus, while each chapter stands on its own, the collection coalesces around interpreting community and listening. Contributors engage with how storytelling encourages recognition of the power of languages and, in so doing, offers alternative expressions of citizenship and knowledge in our communities. The multilingual nature of the workshop itself drove home the significance of language in communicating across epistemologies. In particular, not only did the tireless efforts of a team of Weledeh dialect interpreters facilitate the contributions of Yellowknives Dene Elders, but at several points throughout the workshop the interpreters underlined their role as just that—interpreters, not translators. The translator, conceived thus, is not a transferor of words but a generator of meaning. The role of the interpreter, however, is participatory and underscores her active dialogue with the languages—not simply searching for proximate words but producing meaning that speaks to the relationship of the languages in the moment.

This volume brings together storytellers and "research storytellers" to explore storytelling as a mode of understanding—one that supplies both rich research material and powerful ways of communicating research. While this method of engaging with and thinking about the world is new to some, it is a way of life for others. In this vein, our aim in making this book is to foster in-depth exchange between celebrated storytellers, people who have long experience with different uses and modes of storytelling. Thus, this collection profiles, is inspired by, and draws from Indigenous thinkers rooted in their communities' oral storytelling traditions; non-Indigenous writers, poets, musicians, and filmmakers; and scholars who have encountered storytelling in a substantial dimension of their work and embrace it as part of their teaching practice and research dissemination. Contributors speak to each other, across and through the chapters in this collection, to reveal the various synergies between chapter themes, permitting interaction, rather than juxtaposition, between chapters. The resulting interdisciplinary and cross-cultural dialogue yields important insights in terms of policy-making, activism, meaning, and healing.

Chapters are organized to specifically explore one of three key modes of engagement with storytelling: understanding, sharing, and creation. The chapters range from the autobiographical to the poetic to the scholarly. In the first section of the collection, "Storytelling to Understand," authors draw on both theoretical and empirical work to examine storytelling as a way of knowing. In chapter 1, Leonie Sandercock uses long-form poetry to capture, from a non-Indigenous perspective, the experience of engaging in community-based work with First Nations communities. In chapter 2, Christine Stewart and Jacquie Leggatt actively engage with the visual and audible urban landscape in Edmonton, Alberta, to know the city through its stories. (Readers will find Leggatt's underbridge recordings on Soundcloud.) Exploring the underbridge and the mainly Indigenous people encamped there, the authors attend to the significance of Indigeneity in the city and the (post)colonial state, and to relationships between Indigenous and non-Indigenous people, through the historical and contemporary stories rooted in that place. In both chapters, the authors dig into stories as sources of knowledge and sites for the coming together of diverse world views and perspectives. In chapter 3, Patrick Moore extends this view of stories as he traces the relationship between the use of multiple languages in Kaska narrative performances and the social meanings that such multilingualism reflects. Situating Kaska–English code-switching in the personal histories of individual storytellers and the broader history of relations between Indigenous and non-Indigenous communities in the Yukon, Moore draws attention to the considerable linguistic sophistication that such bilingual narratives require, as well as to dominant ideologies that disregard or disfavour the innovative narrative practices encountered here.

In section 2, "Storytelling to Share," authors demonstrate the power of stories to share knowledge and convey significant lessons, as well as to engage different audiences in knowledge exchange. In chapter 4, Kendra Mitchell-Foster and Sarah De Leeuw explore the ways in which arts-based storytelling practices (sketching, mask making, painting, narrative writing, visual art mapping, and even music) build heartfelt and emotionally resonant relationships between the often disparate communities of First Nations in northern British Columbia, health researchers, and future physicians. Their exploration suggests that arts-based methods and methodologies provide important tools for sharing stories and experiences, a finding that sheds new light on the need for culturally relevant health care and practice and underscores the importance of heartfelt and deeply affected orientations to human well-being. In chapter 5, Jasmine Spencer looks at the role of storytelling in the life of François Mandeville (1878–1952), a Métis-Chipewyan trapper, fur trader, interpreter, and storyteller. A remarkable man with a storied career as a trapper and Hudson's Bay Company trader, Mandeville was also a master navigator and translator, skills that helped him make his way in a challenging landscape of muskeg, lakes, rivers, and boreal forest, not to mention appreciated by traders, colonial agents, and trappers. His affinity for languages and communication also aided him in navigating multiple cultures and world views. In 1928, Mandeville narrated twenty stories to a young Chinese linguist, Li Fang-Kuei, who was seeking to study Dene languages. Containing descriptions of how Indigenous peoples educate their youth, fish, make canoes, tan moosehide, and hunt beaver, these stories are as much about understanding an Indigenous culture and way of life as they are a testament to Mandeville's skill at navigating both the land and cultural difference. Both chapters in this section go beyond story as text to explore the ways in which storytelling takes on many forms as a tool for meaningful communication and engagement.

Finally, in the third section, "Storytelling to Create," one poem and two short memoirs engage with storytelling to produce, or create, knowledge, particularly through explorations of relationship to place. In chapter 6, Rita Wong draws inspiration from the waters surrounding Yellowknife, Northwest Territories, to explore dimensions of community, environmental issues, and water-based ecology. In chapter 7, Bren Kolson offers a magical account of a young girl, growing up in the Northwest Territories, who is introduced to the world beyond her small community through the tales of Old Rawhide, a beloved radio storyteller (based on the late Canadian Broadcasting Corporation host Max Ferguson). Finally, in chapter 8, Zoe Todd explores her own Métis identity by way of her work with Inuvialuit women in Paulatuk, Northwest Territories. All three chapters explore the power of story as a maker of meaning and place, communicating complex themes and ideas through visceral, moving narratives and representation.

Activating the Heart draws upon the power of imagination, creativity, and narrative to stimulate new research, creative works, and community engagement. As a collaborative endeavour, interdisciplinary and cross-cultural engagement remains integral to community building, in and out of academia. This collection connects diverse communities with similar interests in the richness and variety of languages, histories, literatures, geographies, epistemologies, ontologies, spiritual beliefs, ecologies, healing practices, and activism. Moreover, in the spirit of the workshop from which this collection emerges and the tasks set by the Elders present, *Activating the Heart* fosters a reflection on institutional reform, decolonization, at the disciplinary level, to engage Indigenous and non-Indigenous epistemologies in conversation with one another responsibly. This collection encourages innovative ways to recognize through storytelling that, to borrow Jo-Ann Episkenew's words, "the creative process has restorative powers" (2009, 68). With such reflections, we offer this modest contribution to enable further acceptance of the positive value and contributions that creative work has to offer both universities and the communities beyond them.

SECTION ONE

storytelling
to understand

Finding My Way: Emotions and Ethics in Community-Based Action Research with Indigenous Communities

Leonie Sandercock

Prologue

In 2006 I was invited to the town of Burns Lake in north-central British Columbia (BC) by a non-Indigenous anti-racism activist who had seen a documentary I'd just finished about a culturally diverse neighbourhood in Vancouver and the challenges of racism (Attili and Sandercock 2007). I was invited as a filmmaker, as a potential storyteller. But what story or stories needed to be told? After a year of local research (archival, but mostly talking to a lot of folks), I thought the story was about Canada's shocking history of apartheid, expressed through the local history of conflict between Indigenous Carrier people and non-Indigenous settlers. This was a story that posed a major question not just for Burns Lake but for Canada: Given this toxic history, is there a way forward? We conceived the making of a film in and with this deeply divided community as an action research project that would culminate in the careful design of cross-cultural community dialogues that could potentially create a space for healing and reconciliation: what I've since come to describe as a therapeutic planning intervention (see Sandercock and Attili 2013, 2014).

During and beyond this five-year community engagement, it gradually became clear that there was an equally important (to me) parallel story, about educating the heart, about what I've come to call "loving attachment" (Erfan and Sandercock 2012). That is a story in which the researcher's gaze turns inward and asks an unsettling question: In addition to what may have changed in Indigenous/non-Indigenous relations in Burns Lake as a result of

the action research, how did the experience change me? Here are those intersecting stories.

1.
Let's start with the Dark Side!
My profession, vocation, mission,
Planning:
that child of Enlightenment
"linking knowledge to action,"
but whose knowledge, for what actions?
in the public interest, they say,
"managing our co-existence in shared space,"
but for whom?
an apartheid kind of co-existence?

The unpalatable truth:
for all its good intentions
progressive motivations
stories of heroes and heroic projects—
think Robert Moses and his Mephisthophelean
transformations of New York and environs;
or Harlan Bartholomew's Plan for Vancouver
removing the Indians from the city
they don't belong here in 1929,
they belong to the past
beyond the city beyond modernity.

For all its good intentions,
the dirty little secret of the historic record
is self-serving, justice-defying,
status quo–protecting:
not just good intentions gone wrong, thru
lack of knowledge or greed or corruption
(although some of that for sure)
but also deeply implicated as
facilitators of social exclusion

economic deprivation
marginalizing minorities
colonizing Indigenes
perpetrators of structural violence while
"just doing our jobs"
implementing legislation within a colonial system.
Land stolen children stolen
people forced to relocate
for the "administrative convenience" of the DIA
(Dept of Indian Affairs)
or for economic development,
in the national interest, of course.

Land-use policies, bylaws, legal
and bureaucratic exercises of power
structural violence authorized by the state
the ordering and policing of certain bodies
in space:
certain bodies marked as different, as Other,
as lesser, as "not persons"
as a problem to be solved.
Like the "Indian Problem":
that is spatial planning, that is the
Reserve System of Indian Lands
confining Natives to a tiny portion—
less than half of one percent
of their former territories—
of what was becoming the province of BC.
Like the Indian Residential Schools:
that is social planning,
a hundred years of planning
to destroy community and culture,
"to kill the Indian in the Native child,"
to break all bonds of attachment.
Like the Indian Act of 1876:
reducing hitherto sovereign Nations

to "wards of the state,"
that is governance planning.

An official policy of assimilation, using
three technologies of power that together
spell GENOCIDE.

And the worst of it is,
this is not just history.
This is the colonial present.

2.
And I still call myself a planner?

3.
Can planning/planners redeem ourselves
repair the wounds of the past
become an instrument of healing and justice
or is this another in a long line of
professional delusions about so-called
progressive planning?
What new forms of practice might lead to healing
this tragic past?
What do we need to learn?
What do we have to unlearn?
Who do we have to become, to play this role
of decolonizing,
of the profession, its practices, and
most challenging of all,
of our non-Indigenous selves?

4.
And me, specifically,
as opposed to the convenient
yet confusing academic "we":

immigrant Australian working class
white girl PhD-ed and socialized
into Anglo-American academia.
Professor at an early age,
yet still the sense of the impostor.
Class does that, as does Race,
and so many other dividers
that tell us our place.

When only 4% of Australian professors
were women, and I became one of them,
ambivalent academic from the get-go
always thinking I understood what it was
to be a minority, blind
to the contradictions of my own privilege
in the upwardly mobile meritocracy
of the baby boom generation,
always taking the part of the underdog
always the social justice orientation
always the sense of fighting the good fight,
suspicious of accusations of white privilege
when I had never "felt" my privilege.

Identity stories are just
so much more complicated, I told myself,
and conveniently left it at that.

And/yet now in Canada
and beneficiary of research grants,
and an invitation to visit a (to me) remote
northern interior town,
in my depth of immigrant ignorance and
still unacknowledged white privilege and
with all my radical planning baggage intact,
I begin a journey of confronting

Indigenous Canada and,
reluctantly but inevitably,
also myself.

5.
Encountering "the north,"
stereotypes pave the way: the people
suspicious of outsiders
city folks university folks government folks,
maybe all for good reasons.
The landscape, God's Own Country,
lakes rivers mountains wildlife
hunters' paradise no place for sissies
in minus-40 winters and bug-infested summers.
Cowboy mentality and
plenty of Indians to kick around.
You don't have to be in Canada long
to absorb these stereotypes.
Could I leave them behind me
in the closet of the urban townhouse
or would they shadow me
hiding in my back pocket?
Could I find and occupy a space of neutrality?
Should I?

What about my outsiderness
as urban and academic,
which is also an insiderness
in power relations and resources?
Would *anyone* talk openly with me,
Native or non-Native?

What about my ignorance?
How to inhabit a "contact zone" always
already contaminated by history,
teachers and priests

social workers and cops
hell-bent on saving or improving
civilizing or assimilating?

How else but with a "beginner's mind."
Go with humility, prepare, ask,
be prepared to look foolish,
expect to step right in the shit
and to stink some of the time
and be uncomfortable most of the time.

6.
Driving Highway 16 the first time
before I came to know it as locals do
as The Highway of Tears
for the number of Native women who've died
or disappeared hitchhiking it,
driving that three hours
from Prince George it wasn't the beauty
but the devastation of the landscape
that struck me. Swathe after swathe
of pine forest
turned red or grey, dead.
Pine-beetle infestation piercing
the wooden heart of the regional economy.

No big surprise then to see so many
boarded storefronts along the main street;
a bleakness about this town
no obvious sense of civic pride no beautification
just a few half-dead flower baskets
hanging from light poles.
Highway 16 suddenly becoming Main Street
for a mile through the Village of Burns Lake,
Supermarket and pub framing the eastern entrance
cemetery and motel

bookending the western exit
and it felt like most travellers just went
right on through,
nothing visibly attractive or enticing
unless Pioneer Museums are your thing.

My first thought, coffee,
as in I'm not going to get a decent cup here,
and I was right about that,
but not about most of the other thoughts
that came with me from Vancouver. Like
doubting whether healing could be possible
in such an uninspiring setting.
My metropolitan baggage
took time to unpack.

The Village of Burns Lake:
what you see at first seems
just barely enough to make a town
some cheap cafes dilapidated hotel a bank or two
drugstore tacky motels post office
with the Queen's photo,
newspaper office RCMP fortress
community college churches library;
bowling alley closed down movie house
closed down, where do the kids go?
skating rink & skateboard bowl by the lake
spiffy new high school elbowing
the dilapidated old one transformed
into Ts'il Kaz Koh (Burns Lake Band) offices
flying the Mohawk flag (!)
right in your face
on the Highway.

What you don't see at first are the social
and spatial relations off the Highway.

Two Reserves within the town
each of their stories a microcosm
of Canada's race relations:
Ts'il Kaz Koh's Rez on the swamp land
between railroad and lake,
allocated before the Village itself
was laid out and gobbled up a third of the Rez
in one bite after the Transcontinental was built
same time as the Great War,
and more of their land appropriated
after the next world war
for the high school the hospital
some shady housing deals
and then a huge chunk to accommodate
another forced relocation,
Lake Babine Nation moved from their territory
into Burns Lake for the administrative convenience
of the almighty DIA.

Passing thru, you don't see any of that
and you don't see that until recently
Natives walked on one side
of the street and white folks on the other
or that there were race riots on this same
Main Street, hundreds of riled up whites
laying into Natives with baseball bats
or that Natives
weren't allowed in certain stores and
certainly weren't hired.
Apartheid,
more poetically "the two solitudes,"
invisible to the untrained eye.

Invisible to me
until my local guides
opened my white metropolitan eyes.

7.
The project begins
with an invitation
to collaboration
proceeds with co-production
of ethical protocol
mutual give-and-take, building
to mutual learning
negotiating suspicions
mediating mistakes
scoping out the extent
of the welcome the extent
of the project itself.

Film as planning intervention
privileging the past
over the future
creating a space where healing
might begin
if denial could end.
That is the vision.
Telling a story that might shift
the balance between the polarities
of a deeply divided community.

Looking for possibility.

8.
I met him in the Band office
this legendary Chief,
long braids, flint eyes,
said to "eat white folks for breakfast"
warrior reputation
known for confrontation
no hostages taken.

He'd been in a running battle
with Village, Mayor, Settlers,
for twenty years
a battle for stolen land,
recognition, rights, dignity.

The moment of introduction
a decisive moment
words incidental
he didn't look into my eyes but through them
and saw whatever is within.
An undressing of my very being.
My heart rate surged
the desire to be somewhere/anywhere else
was overwhelming.

We went outside for a smoke
some incidental talk then
an invitation.
Come with me.

He took me down to the railway tracks
dividing the Rez from the town
swamp land from high ground.
There's our story.
What do you see?

And so began a field trip
into our mutual history
he the first among many
willing to share story
as teaching, guiding me to see
to feel my hitherto unexplored
white privilege.

His willingness to share
his invitation to family sweat-lodge
ceremonies, his jokey emails,
kept me returning because and
in spite of the bitter taste
of the learning I was experiencing.
Absorbing the guilt of my culture.

9.
So what did I see at the railway tracks?
On one side, the Town side,
a pretty municipal sign
carefully painted proudly announcing
"Welcome to Burns Lake:
Gateway to Tweedsmuir Park."

Across the tracks, on the Rez side,
The Wall.
Words of fury splashed across it
words screaming at a passing train
screaming at town residents
if they cared to look, but didn't
INDIANS HAVE NO RIGHTS IN THIS TOWN!
END APARTHEID NOW
INJUSTICE ANYWHERE IS INJUSTICE
EVERYWHERE!
YOU CAN CONTROL OUR WATER BUT
YOU CAN'T CONTROL OUR SOULS.

The Wall,
separating the homes of those whose
water and sewerage had been turned off
mid-winter year 2000
by the Village, and the homes of those
who had turned it off.

A flashpoint burned into the history
of this town that is not a community
but two solitudes:
Native and non-Native.
A flashpoint that is not ancient history
but twenty-first century.

10.
Thus began my education,
other teachers following.
The women Elders who cried
as they shared what they perceived
as their failures as parents.
And I cried with them
as they told of their humiliations
and deprivations
and separations from family and
community
in Residential School;
the attempts to escape the attempts
to protect siblings the punishments
cruel and brutalizing,
intended to destroy
all bonds of attachment
intended to destroy
community and culture.

The Elder
whose mother refused to teach her
Carrier language because
she would only be punished
for speaking it.
And the terrible shame
of not speaking it.

The Ojibway mental health counsellor,
migrated east to west
body pierced green mohawk hair,
shared a shocking story
of his crime and punishment,
confession and self-criticism,
but above all of healing himself
through connecting to culture,
and now there for the youth, 24/7.

The senior policy advisor
who'd come with his rancher dad
from California via Wyoming
and was changed forever on reading
the Indian Act
of 1876, and still going strong,
and insisted I read it,
who introduced me to the tragic story
of the Cheslatta Carrier people,
evicted from their homelands for
a hydro-aluminum project, they
in the way of our "development."
A half-day in the telling,
my listener's tears flowing,
no way to walk away, forget,
do nothing, feel nothing.

The youth who told me of their shame
simply being born Native,
and the non-Native music teacher
working with those youth to create
their anti-racism song,
and set them on a different path.

The non-Native high school dance teacher
married to the Chief

defying the unspoken rules
broaching the difficult topics
through performance:
Residential Schools, homosexuality, hair,
"Baby step by baby step
so much work to be done
I'm just a small part of it
but I have to do my part."

And the two (ex-)Mennonites:
one with a business degree
running the Community Forest and hanging
with the anti-racism crowd,
challenged by the Mayor to explain
his choice of friends,
his answer simply
"I agree with their values."

The other, the anti-racism activist,
who'd invited me here to witness
the stories, introduced me to Right
Left and Centre, Native and non-Native,
believer and non-believer,
never told me what to think
and above all taught me
the true meaning of partnership
between Indigenous and non-Indigenous Canada.

The dance of getting to know
taking the time many stumbles
missed steps missed cues
not listening not watching
being made fun of kindly
observing other ways of teaching
discarding preconceptions
discovering three dimensions.

11.
A process unfolds by mutual consent
I am outsider interpreter ally
and critical friend
turning their stories into film
potentially healing potentially
explosive addressing apartheid
not sugar-coated.

Film as inquiry
exploration meaning making
film with a purpose, a process
moving toward possibility—
toward dialogue
the process itself advancing
the purpose because and despite
the conflict.

A year of research
four months filming
four years editing and returning
screenings for feedback
corrections additions suggestions.

Four months designing
the space of community dialogue
advised by the Main Characters
heroes villains everywo/man
Mayor Chiefs Elders
Youth teachers police.

Training local youth and Elders
as facilitators,
organizing music and food and
counsellors, just in case,

so much psychological wreckage
in colonization's wake.

Structuring the dialogues:
What moved you most
in this/your story?
Is the past still present?
What should be done?
What will you do?

Own your emotions but
own your history too
and be prepared to see it
thru Others' eyes and emotions.
Leave all defences at the door
and enter the screening
your lives on display
your hearts and minds open.

12.
The dialogues begin:
talking circles spirit feather
soft voices angry voices
silences tears shock shame
surprise relief catharsis
hope: both cautious and feisty
visions: of moving forward together.

13.
Was there some healing across
the cultural divide
through this planning intervention?

What does transformation look like?

There is no metric,
just the stories
the voices of hope.
Post-dialogue questionnaires,
for what they're worth,
showed changes in attitude:
a desire to get to know "the Other"
shock at living in ignorance so long
about the lives of "the Other"
shame at believing the dominant narrative
about "the Other."
The quality of listening and engagement,
remarkable.
The energy for change,
palpable.
Some of the Native youth started
a Facebook page for change in their community.
One of the non-Native youth ran for Mayor
and won, at age twenty-one,
and embodies the spirit
of healing reconciliation justice.

There was recognition,
there was empowerment,
there is the beginning of a new story
about the need to move forward together
in full recognition of past injustice
and the need to build a new web
of social relationships
and an understanding that the hope
is with the youth.

14.
What did I learn about planning
in deeply divided communities?

That to address collective
trauma amnesia denial,
we need collective forums,
public spaces for working thru
historic and ongoing injustices
for bearing witness for recognition
for taking responsibility
for bringing the past into conversation
with the present and future
in spaces carefully designed
to protect the vulnerable
and unsettle the powerful.

Colonial planning knew what was best
for its "subjects" and reduced them to dependency,
progressive planning sought to abolish
cultural difference in the name of equality,
and postmodern planning sought inclusion
thru recognition of difference
but didn't recognize
claims to rights, title, sovereignty.

How then to imagine
a decolonizing planning project?

As a way of being,
starting from a depth
of not knowing
humble open-hearted caring
listening more than talking
not helping or solving,
but supporting
and always and only when invited.

Reversing the gaze,
interrogating our own institutions
observing our own daily actions
for the all-but-guaranteed
evidence of paternalism
disguised as expertise.

Moving beyond guilt and
beyond craving for legitimacy
to a politics and praxis
of love and justice:
knowing love is not enough and
that justice means making noise
when I see injustice,
a research/practice
respectful and fearless
caring and courageous
standing alongside
walking together, working
face-to-face.

That's what being an ally means.
But where does this politics begin?

Surely at home.

15.
So what did I learn
about myself?
Myself in relation
myself and my profession
myself and my privilege?

How/was I transformed?

Drawn to this way of working
from a career-long feeling of Lack:
in those critical arguments
and assured pronouncements
about who and what matters,
those devastating judgements
that crush or boost,
intellectual power games
gatekeeping the establishment.
I've done all of that and
for some of it, am ashamed
for being good at
playing that game.
The Lack that has no name
but resides in the body and psyche
as wound,
wound whose only healing
is *activating the heart.*

Working in partnership
in community
shows me/us a different way
of being in the world.
You/I cannot be in community
without loving attachment
humble open-hearted vulnerable
patient critical and hopeful
listening thru silence
walking lightly speaking softly:
without these and more
I will always be suspect,
undeserving of trust.

The Lack now lives in me
as a vow
to honour this way of being

to make the connections
to all my relations,
everywhere.
I don't always keep this vow
and at such times
I disappoint myself and know
I am ethically suspect.

How to practise loving attachment?
The chemistry of attachment
is relationship.
The ethics of attachment
is reciprocity.
The work of attachment
starts from learning
the meaning and practice of respect.

And I keep stumbling upon
new ways of being disrespectful,
in spite of good intentions.
Those good intentions are
the biggest trap, leading to
self-righteous indignation
instead of humble self-questioning.

My great good fortune
are the teachers
who don't give up on me,
with varying degrees of gentle patience
and tough love
they are showing me the way.

Inching my way out of ignorance.
Heart activated.
Full of gratitude.
A work in progress.

Epilogue

For all of the power of the experience of working in partnership in that community, for the unforgettable experience of activating the heart, for the lessons learned about how to work with First Nations, the ultimate and hardest lesson was in returning to my own community, the university, and asking some tough questions about what I/we were teaching and in what ways we were deeply and blindly entrenched in ongoing colonial practices. I began to ask about the decolonizing work that needed to be done in my own backyard. Which I think is Paulette Regan's message in her provocative book, *Unsettling the Settler Within* (Regan 2011).

My backyard is the University of British Columbia, which sits on the traditional, ancestral, and unceded territory of the Musqueam people. The question staring me in the face on my return: Why isn't my School (of Community and Regional Planning) talking about any of this? I started to talk about it and was encouraged by the director of SCARP, Penny Gurstein, to make some recommendations about curriculum reform. I opened a conversation with our Musqueam neighbors, hoping they would want to be involved. Three years later, SCARP is in a formal partnership with the Musqueam Indian Band in the design and delivery of an Indigenous Community Planning program within our master's degree. We currently have twelve students in this program, half of them Indigenous. The students spend half of their second year working on Reserve with First Nations communities on aspects of comprehensive community planning. I co-teach a new core course (Indigenous Community Planning: Ways of Being, Knowing and Doing) with a Musqueam Elder and an Indigenous doctoral student, Lyanna Patrick.

Acknowledgements

While this poetic essay is a very personal reflection on my own learning journey, I was not alone on this journey. I was accompanied by my research partner, co-filmmaker, and friend for life, Giovanni Attili. This was our project for five years. Vanni, I will never forget the look of stunned shock on your face on the return flight after your first trip to Burns Lake. I think we were both asking ourselves, "WTF have we gotten ourselves into here?" And "How on earth can we make any sense of any of this?" We got to know each other in a very deep way, warts and all, through the sharing of this indelible experience. Mille grazie, Vanni.

Towards the end of the project we were each gifted a blanket by the then Chief of the Ts'il Kaz Koh Nation, Rob Charlie, who thanked us "for taking the time to get to know us." Rob and family, I hope you know what a privilege that was.

Special thanks to my mentors: Ted Jojola, Gerry Oleman, Rob Charlie, Corrina Leween, and Norma-Jean McLaren.

And immense gratitude to Libby Porter and Aftab Erfan for their critical reading of earlier versions of this personal reflection.

A Note on Sources

This poetic essay/prose poem has been informed by many scholars whose works are listed below and whose words and thought fragments have found their way into my essay, as well as by the people of Burns Lake, the Ts'il Kaz Koh Nation, and the Cheslatta Carrier Nation. For a more traditional social science analytical account of our work in Burns Lake, see Sandercock and Attili (2012, 2013, 2014). For information about the film we made, *Finding Our Way*, see Attili and Sandercock (2010); www.mongrel-stories.com; and www.movingimages.ca.

Bibliography

Attili, Giovanni, and Leonie Sandercock. 2010. *Finding Our Way*. 90-minute documentary. Vancouver: Moving Images.

Barry, Janice, and Libby Porter. 2012. "Indigenous Recognition in State-Based Planning Systems: Understanding Textual Mediation in the Contact Zone." *Planning Theory* 11 (2): 170–87. https://doi.org/10.1177/1473095211 427285.

Deloria, Vine, Jr. 1999. "A Flock of Anthros." In *Spirit and Reason: The Vine Deloria Jr. Reader*, 123–26. Golden, CO: Fulcrum Publishing.

de Leeuw, Sarah. 2004. *Unmarked: Landscapes along Highway 16*. Edmonton, AB: NeWest Press.

Erfan, Aftab. 2013. "An Experiment in Therapeutic Planning: Learning with the Gwa'sala-'Nakwaxda'xw First Nations." PhD diss., University of British Columbia.

Erfan, Aftab, and Leonie Sandercock. 2012. "Plato's Lacunae: On the Value of Loving Attachment in Community-Based Planning Research and Practice." *Planning Theory and Practice* 13 (4): 620–27.

Friedmann, John. 1973. *Retracking America*. New York: Doubleday Anchor.

———. 1987. *Planning in the Public Domain: From Knowledge to Action*. Princeton, NJ: Princeton University Press.

Graveline, Fyre Jean. 2000. "Circle as Methodology: Enacting an Aboriginal Paradigm." *International Journal of Qualitative Studies in Education* 13 (4): 361–70. https://doi.org/10.1080/095183900413304.

Healey, Patsy. 2007. *Collaborative Planning*. 2nd ed. London: Macmillan.

hooks, bell. 2000. *All about Love: New Visions*. New York: Harper Collins.

Irlbacher-Fox, Stephanie. 2009. *Finding Dahshaa. Self-Government, Social Suffering, and Aboriginal Policy in Canada*. Vancouver: UBC Press.

Jojola, Ted. 2008. "Indigenous Planning: An Emerging Paradigm." *Canadian Journal of Urban Research* 17 (1 Supplement): 37–47.

Kovach, Margaret. 2009. *Indigenous Methodologies: Characteristics, Conversations, Contexts*. Toronto: University of Toronto Press.

Littlebear, Leroy. 2009. "Jagged Worldviews Colliding." In *Reclaiming Indigenous Voice and Vision*, edited by Marie Battiste, 77–85. Vancouver: UBC Press.

Marris, Peter. 1975. *Loss and Change*. London: Routledge and Kegan Paul.

Nussbaum, Martha. 2001. *Upheavals of Thought. The Intelligence of Emotions*. Cambridge: Cambridge University Press. https://doi.org/10.1017/CBO 9780511840715.

Pelias, Ron. 2004. *A Methodology of the Heart*. New York: Altamira Press.

Porter, Libby. 2010. *Unlearning the Colonial Cultures of Planning*. London: Ashgate.

Pratt, Mary Louise. 1992. *Imperial Eyes: Travel Writing and Transculturation*. London: Routledge. https://doi.org/10.4324/9780203163672.

Regan, Paulette. 2011. *Unsettling the Settler Within*. Vancouver: UBC Press.

Sandercock, Leonie. 2003. *Cosmopolis 2: Mongrel Cities of the 21st Century*. London: Continuum.

Sandercock, Leonie, and Giovanni Attili. 2012. "Unsettling a Settler Society: Film, Phronesis and Collaborative Planning in Small Town Canada." In *Real Social Science*, edited by Bent Flyvbjerg, Todd Landman, and Sanford Schram, 137–66. Cambridge: Cambridge University Press. https://doi.org/10.1017/CBO9780511719912.010.

———. 2013. "The Past as Present: Film as a Community Planning Intervention in Native/Non-Native Relations in British Columbia, Canada."

In *Reclaiming Indigenous Planning*, edited by Ryan Walker, Ted Jojola, and David Natcher, 60–93. Montreal and Kingston: McGill-Queen's University Press.

————. 2014. "Changing the Lens: Film as Action Research and Therapeutic Planning Practice." *Journal of Planning Education and Research* 34 (1): 19–29. https://doi.org/10.1177/0739456X13516499.

Smith, Linda Tuhiwai. 2012. *Decolonizing Methodologies*, 2nd ed. London: Zed Books.

Stanger-Ross, Jordan. 2008. "Municipal Colonialism in Vancouver: City Planning and the Conflict Over Indian Reserves." *Canadian Historical Review* 89 (4): 541–80. https://doi.org/10.3138/chr.89.4.541.

Wilson, Shawn. 2008. *Research Is Ceremony*. Halifax, NS: Fernwood Publishing.

CHAPTER TWO

Notes from the UNDERBRIDGE

Christine Stewart with Jacquie Leggatt

FIGURE 2.1   "Listen." Les Danyluk, photographer

These notes are a series of observations made in the second phase of the Underbridge Project, an ongoing study of a place in Edmonton, Alberta, under the Mill Creek Bridge at Whyte Avenue. The central and difficult question of the project is how I, as a white settler person, might be here, in Edmonton, in Canada, on this colonized land, in a good way. So far, each installment reflects my thinking, my reading, and my listening at a particular time; each is part of the trajectory of my life on Treaty 6 territory. In the first installment, "Propositions from under Mill Creek Bridge" (Stewart 2015), I attempted a reading of the underbridge, noting, photographing, and interpreting the signs and symbols found there.[1] The work here considers the problems with and limitations of that particular reading and the limitations of reading in general. Here, I consider a practice of listening as a potentially more precise and holistic way of attending to place. I also reconsider my initial reading of biologist of Jakob von Uexküll in "Propositions from under Mill Creek Bridge" and trace the recording work that I did with composer Jacquie Leggatt as a component of this practice of listening. The piece concludes with Jacquie Leggatt's "Compositional Notes from the Underbridge and Listening Exercises," an auditory movement through the underbridge of Mill Creek.

Like the first underbridge piece, this is a work in progress, rife with its own failures and flaws, and I alone am responsible for any errors that may be found here.

Note 1 Under the Bridge
The Underbridge Project began in Edmonton, Alberta, in the fall of 2007. I was new to the city, and I rode my bike under the Mill Creek Bridge in Mill Creek Ravine each morning on my way to work. What greeted me each day was striking and, at first, difficult to grasp. A recent oil boom, and the resulting high cost of housing, had brought inner-city residents south, across the North Saskatchewan River, to the ravine, and under the bridge. Some slept on the cement ledges just under the bridge deck; others camped along the creek. In the cold fall mornings, smoke rose from campfires, and the small brown creek glistened. The scene was pastoral and apocalyptic, and, as I came to understand, it was very Canadian. Most of the people living in the ravine and under the bridge at that time were Indigenous, and many would have been nêhiyaw (Cree)—on their traditional territory, Treaty 6—home and yet homeless.

For the most part, above the ravine, life for the homeowners, joggers, dog walkers, and cyclists went on as usual that fall. The state of emergency in which the sleepers existed was exceptional only to the extent to which it disturbed the people who lived in the houses and condos on the edge of the park. On weekday mornings, people called in to the local CBC radio program and complained about the number of people living in the ravine.

That year, as I rode my bike through the ravine and under the Mill Creek Bridge, I encountered ravens, thick dust, oil slicks, creeping thistle, river rock, a shopping cart, a diaper, a walker, car exhaust, mud, wild roses, brown creek, the warm steam of sewage, coyote songs pitched to the ambulance sirens on the road above, and many sleepers. It was there that I began to wonder what it meant to be here, in this ravine, in this city, in this country. As a non-Indigenous person deeply embedded and implicated in white settler ideology, I wondered, in a way for the first time, who is that I that I am when I am here?

What forces formed this I, here—its sense and stories of land and entitlement, its gaze?

There is no place more private or more public than the word "I." We don't know where it has been; we know exactly where it has been: in a million mouths, on as many tongues, next to teeth, covered in spit. Passed on, within a Western European context, there is no other English word (it is barely a word) that is more constricted, constraining, suspect, and conforming.

"It is not strictly the 'I' that speaks, and nor is it the living individual." (Agamben 2002, 117)

That fall, I wondered how that I, riding under that bridge, on those mornings, could understand what she found there.

Note 2 Jakob von Uexküll and the Anthropological Machine

Searching for ways of seeing and reading, I (that is and is not mine) was initially compelled by the early twentieth-century biologist Jakob von Uexküll's concept of the environment as a collection of spheres, or *Umwelten*, constituted by animal species. The idea of the *Umwelt* seemed to offer a productive way of considering the underbridge and the myriad worlds that existed there.

According to Uexküll (2010), the Umwelt is an environment that a species of animal perceives and inhabits according to its own cognitive apparatus.

Each species pays attention to specific marks or "carriers of meaning," existing side by side, engaged with each other in deeply reciprocal relations (140), despite, as Giorgio Agamben (2004) notes in his reading of Uexküll, the fact that these infinitely varied worlds are uncommunicating and exclusive (40). That is, according to Uexküll, a spider creates a web perfectly designed to catch a fly (it is fly-like), but otherwise, the spider is oblivious to the fly's world (Agamben 2004, 43), as is the fly to the Umwelt of the spider (42). Engaged with each other in patterns of connection and obliviousness, these environments are composed of living subjects equally perfect and bound together, as Uexküll writes, working as if in the musical score of a symphony (Uexküll 2010, 245n5).

Within the discipline of Western European science, Uexküll's biological framework radically shifted the idea of evolutionary progress and vertical thinking towards a spatial and horizontal biology (Agamben 2004, 40). The consequences of this shift were far-reaching—from biological studies to philosophy. For Agamben, this development challenges the centrality of the human and resituates the Western European frameworks that have constituted the human (and the subject I) as a negotiated binary of human and animal, of animal and human—determined (and redetermined) by the shifting designations of who or what is most violent, most bloody (38).

However, Uexküll's later adjustments to his theory would reinstate this binary. In the afterword to a 2010 edition of Uexküll's *Foray into the World of Animals and Humans*, Geoffrey Winthrop-Young (2010, 225–43) notes the "dangerous" slippages that occur later in Uexküll's theory when the biologist ascribes different Umwelts to women, nations, regions, and professions, particularly artisanal occupations passed on from father to son.[2] Uexküll's shift from interspecies to intraspecies Umwelten, including social human groups, is based on his idea of "organicism"; that is, Uexküll attributes to the body a static natural state, organically ruled by a central control system (Winthrop-Young 2010, 224). By extension, he suggests that an authentic nation, social group, or profession would also be ruled in such a way, with its Umwelt expressing a fixed and essential dimension. For Uexküll, there were also communities that existed outside of these authentic systems and that threatened the natural and authentic course of events—particularly, secular Jewish individuals and communities.[3] According to Uexküll, secular Judaism manifested an *Umweltvergessenheit* (a forgetfulness of Umwelt) and infected authentic ways of life with the toxicity of modernity (Winthrop-Young 2010, 229). Here, Uexküll's conceptual framework reinforces the modern anthropological machine that Agamben seeks to undermine. Furthermore, Uexküll's later version of his theory creates another hierarchy, producing an outside through the exclusion of an inside (Agamben 2004, 37) and rendering Jewishness outside the system of the human Umwelt.

Uexküll's notions of authenticity and preordination fail to support his initial radical proposition of life as a horizontal composition. It is important to keep this failure in mind in the context of the Underbridge Project. What conceptual framework ever exists apart from the systematic and normalized violence of its time? How might I address my own obliviousness to other forms of being, my own attachments to "the authentic," without re-engaging in the brutality of the Western European anthropological machine? How might I negotiate the unknowingness in which I find myself as I encounter the complex communities of the underbridge? How might I learn to respectfully acknowledge my relations and my obligations, navigating the dense and entwined materialities of bodies—acknowledging and opening to the silences—I encounter there? How might I learn to attend to the infinite circumferences of being, interactive, reciprocal, and unseeing, expressed in a vast composition of relations?

These questions challenge the privileged premises of seeing and reading in my earlier study, "Propositions from under Mill Creek Bridge." Colonial concepts of illumination are fundamental to the very systems I wish to resist.

> Mirrour of grace and Majestie diuine,
> Great Lady of the greatest Isle, whose light
> Like Phoebus lampe throughout the world doth shine,
> Shed thy faire beames ...
> (Spenser 1909, *The Faerie Queene*, bk. 1, lines 29–32)

Is it possible to reconfigure a practice of attention that is mired in the criminal imbroglio of Western European colonization? How might I be here?

Perhaps I could listen, practise the possibilities of listening—not as a conventional researcher, a detached subject, but as a body next to other bodies, "all ears"? Might I learn notes of significance? Welcome the indiscernible, accepting other compositions, and other frameworks of reference?

Note 3 Sound Silence Noise

In the winter of 2011, moving away from the practice of reading to develop a different practice of attention, a poetics of listening, I began to work with Vancouver composer Jacquie Leggatt on an acoustic practice of listening.

We began by considering the acoustic sensibility that emerged from the World Soundscape Project, founded by R. Murray Schafer in the late 1960s. In this work, Schafer resists privileging sight over sound and espouses an anti-visual sensibility, defining "seeing as analytical and reflective, and sound as active and generative" (LaBelle 2006, 195). Schafer's work centres on acoustic ecologies, the complex acoustics of specific places. However, in his recordings, he tends to distinguish and privilege sound over noise, defining noise as urban and lo-fi and sound as natural and hi-fi. For Schafer, noise imposes and interrupts; it disturbs the body, and disrupts society and the environment. Sound, on the other hand, is soothing, with low, ambient tones and discrete measures that merge with clarity (LaBelle 2006, 202). As noise corrodes and contaminates, sound has the potential to soothe the fragmented back into the whole; it allows us to proceed without pain (202).

Schafer's distinctions between sound and noise seemed to us to share something with Uexküll's notion of authenticity. Repulsed by the implications of Uexküll's harmonious symphony, and wary of Schafer's terms, we wanted to consider the acoustics of our relations, of reciprocity, of silence and points of unknowing, in a study of place. And so, we went back under the bridge.

Note 4 Recording

Next to the huge cement piers, to the thin trees and the creek, under the bridge, noise envelops and assaults us. Wearing Jacquie's earphones, holding the Sony recorder, we encounter layers of sound, meetings of lives: dog, jogger, stone, water, car, bird, two men, yelling on the bridge deck above, fighting, then kissing, then laughing. A bird calls through the traffic. At first, the audibility, this acute perception amplified by the earphones, is too much. Noise swarms the listening body—from behind, from above, from below. The ears resist, strain anxiously for comfort, for "natural" soothing sounds, for birdsongs over traffic, over the men's voices. But it all keeps coming, intimate, too public, too private, shattering, and there are no birdsongs, anyway. Only bird noise, bird sounds, world sounds. The eyes close; the I shifts and is shaken. The fast breath of the perceiving body roars in with its own insistent audibility. The body is submerged in its own physicality, in its immediate proximity (surrounded) with the materiality of sound. The ears can't and won't block the siren, the car alarm, the booming truck, the ragged breath, the coughing, coughing body; each noise enters, moves through, and emerges.

Note 5 Aisthetikos Audibilis

Writer Erín Moure (2009) considers how the word "aesthetic" comes from the Greek *aisthetikos* 'of sense perception' and, in Latin, is linked to the root of the word "audible" (29). That is, late Latin *audibilis*, from Latin *audire* 'to hear,' is akin to Greek *aisthanesthai* 'to perceive.'[4] "Anæsthetic comes from anaist-hetos (insensible), not-perceiving," Moure writes. "If we are not perceiving the audible ... we are anæsthetized"—numbed (29). For Moure, by attending to the audible, we allow slippage and resistance to the centrifugal pull of the centre; our attentiveness to sound in language breaks the gaze, shatters the specular, and contests the bogus solidity of the subject (29). Sound artist Salomé Voegelin also notes the effect of the audible on the self, claiming that seeing is always (in) a metaposition. In listening, there is no place where "I am not simultaneously with the heard" (Voegelin 2010, xii).

And in the cacophony of the underbridge, Jacquie and I hear clearly that the sounds are not symphonic, not harmonious. Nor are they hi-fi, composed of clear or discrete sounds, as in Schafer's definitions. The sounds of the underbridge are rhythmic and raucous; they are clamorous. Our developing sense of audibility challenges notions of the authentic and the natural. Our listening ears are rife with discord, disruption; we cannot proceed without pain. Nor can anyone else who spends time under the bridge. Here, we are increasingly drawn into a vast and shifting arena of sound. As listeners, we must prick up our ears and tune into the diapason—"the entire range of unfiltered sound" (Kahn 1999, 9). Under the bridge we encounter this range. Uninvited. Unfiltered. Human shriek, bird gurgle, helicopter surge, insect zing: a strange rhythm gathers; tones resonate and expand.

For sound artist LaBelle (2006), this urban soundscape is the desired range: noise "emphasiz[es] ... the outer skin ... the profane" (210). Citing Paul Heggert's "The Politics of Noise," LaBelle argues that "'noise deforms, reconfigures ... dissipates, mutates' rather than unifies or makes whole" (210). However, as LaBelle (2010b) notes in "Sound as Hinge," noise is also healing—where noise "splits apart," it also "mends" and allows for new relations, for unexpected and "emergent communit[ies]" (1–2). Under the bridge, this healing (profane, disrupting, mending, splitting) makes sense. We note the complex dynamics, the points of connection: dog chain to dog; walker to sleeper to stone rattle; magpie to wheel gravel to rough water. In listening, we divide and recombine as subjects, mending and merging in new relations. Noise emerges as sound; noise has a musical beauty and body in its materiality and its relationality with the world. Its disruption is powerful—and maybe even healing, in that it places the listener in her present, accepting, attending to what is, to unexpected points of connection, of access and meaning. Unexpected and possible communities manifest a strange(r) beauty.

And this practice of listening aligns us in a spatial expanse of noise. It engages us in the material boundaries of being. As listeners, Jacquie and I are not confined to the limits of our own materiality—we are informed by our sonic relations, the sounds that resonate within the cavities of our bones and skull. Our listening practice encompasses difficulty and dissonance and the shifting communities of bodies. As LaBelle (2006) writes, "acoustical events are social: in multiplying and expanding space, sound necessarily generates listeners and a multiplicity of acoustical 'viewpoints'" (x). Expanding acoustically in space, generating listeners, the underbridge is a social place—not liminal but integral, communal. But, while the space might be communal, what are the ethics of listening here, like this, with earphones on and recorder held ready? We are careful not to record the voices of particular people—we capture only the ambient sounds of the underbridge—but is this actually different from my previous practice of looking? Have we been invited here to listen and to hear in this way?

Note 6 The Audibility of Topology

Our practice shifts again when Jacquie and I attend the Activating the Heart Workshop in Dettah with the Weledeh Yellowknives Dene community near Yellowknife in June 2012. Here, we gather on the edge of the Great Slave Lake, Tinde'e, in a community of about 250 people. The brilliant water of the bay, Weledeh-Cheh, moves over the flat, wide shore rocks. A raven flies overhead, clatters across the tin roof, and calls. Around the big table, discussions are simultaneously translated into Dene and English. Here, we are given earphones; here, we are invited to listen; we are expected to listen, simultaneously, to both languages. This process is dissonant and confusing, exhausting and soothing, painful and beautiful. The Elders are clear that we must take care to listen to the land, to its stories, and to the stories of the people from that land in their language. This is our obligation.

Later, I learn how this obligation extends back to Edmonton, amiskwaci-wâskahikan 'Beaver Hills House,' to Treaty 6 land, to pêhonân 'the meeting place,' to the underbridge. Walking by the North Saskatchewan River, just below the University of Alberta, Dwayne Donald, Papaschase scholar, asks us to listen for the Cree (nêhiyaw) names of the places, the stories, the stones, to develop a practice of listening that seeks a history, a relationship that acknowledges the binding agreements of treaty (personal communication during River Walk, January 2013). We are asked to engage with the Indigenous communities and nations of this place—the Îyâhé Nakoda (Stoney Nakoda), nêhiyaw, Niitsitapi, Métis—to know the stories of the land and our own specific obligations to Treaty 6. Our responsibility to listen to the history of this land also reaches to Jacquie's home in Vancouver, where other nations and histories prevail: Squamish, Musqueam, and Tsleil-Waututh. Our obligations extend across Canada, across Turtle Island, to other Indigenous communities, to their languages, and to the life-sustaining land. This range of audibility originates in and is determined by specific topologies; it requires our attention, and we are bound by the historical and material consequences of this place and its names.

Note 7 Baffled

As non-Indigenous inhabitants of a place ravaged by colonization, as suspect researchers of the underbridge, we are obliged to hear and to be here (specifically and materially) in an attentive way, seeking historical and present-day points of relationship, working to acknowledge the extent of our responsibilities and obligations, past and present, extensive and audible.

Note 8 The Underbridge

Where the Mill Creek Bridge intersects with the Mill Creek Ravine, it leaves a raw and exposed edge of environmental degradation, poverty, and human displacement, determined and regulated. The underbridge is an example of and a metaphor for the foundations of Canada. Canada is land scarred by the extraction of resources, by development. It is a place inhabited by displaced people. What are our connections to the demarcations so clearly articulated here? What is our connection to this city, this land of malls and big trucks? Under the bridge is ugly: dust and shit. Under the bridge is beautiful: goosefoot,[5] raven wing, and resourceful sleepers. Turn into the cool gloom of the underbridge. Stop in the dark; listen. Be drawn into places of indiscernibility, gaps in our understanding, our education, and our experience, our hearing. Be drawn to places we cannot fully know. How can we know what we do not know? The links here are tenuous and intense, intimate and civic, local, national, and global. There are hundreds, thousands, of other underbridges in this world—colonized places of debris fields,[6] wounded, appropriated earth, displaced Indigenous communities.

The underbridge is a place and an allegory, surpassing its signification with a dense, complex, and generative materiality. Attending acoustically to the underbridge tunes us in to layers of time and presence, to old and new relations—layers of place and absence materialize:

kâhasiniskâk,[7] place of stones, buffalo trail,[8] a dense growth of trees and brush,[9] shanty town (Dwayne Donald, personal correspondence, 1 November 2012), coal mine, abattoir (Monto 2013), coyote den, railway—the matter of this place; the details of its histories, silenced and spoken.

Note 9 Sound Files

At SoundCloud.com, playlist "Notes from the Underbridge," you can find several examples of our listening practice. The collection contains ten unprocessed files, which were recorded under the bridge, and "Mill Creek Quilt 1," which was played in Yellowknife for the Activating the Heart Conference. In "Mill Creek Quilt 1," Jacquie runs the recordings through her computer, loops, splices, and places one sound next to another. These files are archives and aesthetic gatherings, aesthetic perceptions of audibilities. They are sound stories that resonate with and locate the listening body. In them, we are next to: sound brings us into a direct physical relation with our environment. Sound brings us 'round to ourselves, dissolving the edges of our material boundaries, and merges us with other bodies.

To listen to noise that interrupts, that imposes itself indiscriminately, that disturbs the body, that disrupts society and the environment, and that cannot proceed without pain, is a practice that encourages the listener to be beside other circumferences of life—not through possession or control of knowing ("that is a meaningful sound"; "that is a meaningless noise"), not through a determination of authentic and inauthentic, but through an attentiveness. In attending, we attempt to be present in and to, listening to and for points of relation, points of connection, for the possible musicality of these relations—a resting next to, a noting of, a respect for. This was our prepositional acoustic mode of attention, and later, with the guidance of Elders, Indigenous scholars, and knowledge keepers, we listened again.

Note 10 Prepositional Listening

Not a multiplicity of disconnected viewpoints but a multiplicity of viewpoints that are, in themselves, relations—these relations connect Jacquie and me as we work to become attentive subjects in this place, here, hearing, under the bridge manifesting in time, white, settled and settling, unsettled and unsettling.

The more time we spend here, on this land, under this bridge, the more we realize how much we do not know, that there are worlds we silence. As Uexküll excises Jewish communities from his harmonious symphony, who and what do we, as inheritors of a white settler culture and ideology, continually and collectively ignore, obfuscate, and even eradicate?

The city of Edmonton, the country of Canada, the white settler subject, is built on the blood and land of nations, communities, families, and individuals. White settler culture manages and maintains this history with a particular oblivescence. In this city, the histories of the Indigenous nations are not always easy to find. Often, more prevalent are the stories of industry, of capitalism (resource extraction and land development), and of the white communities that established and maintain these systems. But under the bridge, after Dettah, this forgetting is impossible to maintain. We are reminded of the stories that we have never been told. We are compelled to listen in an ethical, perceptive capacity. We are compelled to find a way to be here, to create a poetics of attention in order to locate what we cannot remember.

To try to listen, against obliviousness, against the violence of white settler amnesia, against the violence of selective Eurocentric remembering. To move towards remembering, to move against, away from forgetting, to be before listening, under and above, for the sake of being here, to intensify, to beseech, to obsecrate, to entreat, "from ob- for the sake of + sacrāre to hold in reverence; see sacred."[10]

To be against Canada as a construction of white settler ideology, against Canada as a collective and purposeful place of forgetting, is to challenge standard accounts of reality. When we listen under the bridge, as we have been instructed, we learn that during a boom in the oil industry, many inner-city residents of Edmonton migrate south, across the North Saskatchewan River, to the Mill Creek Ravine, to live under the Mill Creek Bridge. We learn that a strong oil economy means that the cost of housing goes up and homelessness increases. When the economy weakens, rents lower and homelessness usually decreases, because it becomes easier for people on social assistance to find housing. We learn about land theft, a broken treaty, and that in a capitalist, colonial society, a history of theft and a baseline of deprivation are requisite. In this country, there is always someone sleeping under the bridge: in summer and in winter; home and not home.

These days, the topology of the ravine remains pastoral and apocalyptic. The precarity of life under the bridge is accepted by the people who use the ravine as a place of beauty, for recreation or relaxation. This is the norm; despite our developing listening practice, this is our norm, oblivious, obliviating. Our life here is a process and system of active obliterations. We are told that Canada is a good and decent country. We use terms like "postcolonial," and we normalize conditions of devastating poverty. We accept inconceivable rates of incarceration, both of Indigenous adults into the prison system and of Indigenous children into the child welfare system. There are moments when we ask ourselves, how could this happen here? During the news coverage of Attawapiskat, for example, we were shocked by the conditions we saw, which the United Nations identified as comparable to those in the "world's poorest communities" (Mackrael 2011). But, in fact, these conditions constitute Canada as the country has existed so far. Canada and its wealth are built on land and resource theft, on the desecration of original and sacred agreements of sharing, on violations of our treaty obligations. This is what it means to be here: the oppression of Indigenous peoples and their nations through dispossession, community dislocation, violent administrative systems of abuse, isolation, scientific experimentation, genocide, attempted genocide, and government-approved amnesia—to be here is to be forgetful and forgetting, and to enforce the violence of this forgetfulness on others.

Note 11 Resonance

In 1997, in *Delgamuukw v. British Columbia*, the Supreme Court of Canada ruled that oral histories are as important as written testimony, and the necessity of listening is pulled into the legal fray.[11] This ruling and the vibrant presence of orally relayed Indigenous histories challenge Eurocentric understandings of truth and history.

In "Understanding Treaty 6: An Indigenous Perspective," nêhiyaw lawyer Sharon Venne situates the necessity of listening within the context of nêhiyaw identity, the nêhiyaw nation, its history, and the history of Treaty 6:

> When the Elders come together, the stories begin to flow. One Elder alone has many stories, but when a number of Elders are placed in the same room, the stories multiply. Together, the Elders tell a story of a nation. Narrative is a powerful method for teaching many things, including the history of an oral people. The key is to listen … From early childhood, an Indigenous person learns to listen to the Elders and eventually listening becomes an acquired skill. (Venne 1997, 174)

Note 12 Resonance

In "Feeding Sublimity: Embodiment in Blackfoot Experience," Ryan Heavy Head (2005) argues that in Blackfoot cosmology, in áístomatoo'p, "the individual is not at all 'closed' to its environmental Other—but rather permeable and inseparable, even indistinguishable from it, for that environment is the very physical and conceptual stuff that comprises the organism itself, the energy that courses through, transforming and shaping it" (98). In this view, the individual exists in a metonymic, paradigmatic system, as an event or phenomenon in and of the wider socio-ecosystem (98).

Accordingly, under the bridge, on Treaty 6 land, as listeners attending to the requests of the Elders at Dettah, to the nêhiyaw scholars and communities in Edmonton and beyond, we are composed of, bound to, and permeable to the world's materiality, inhabited and formed by its relations, listening to it through our own strange participatory and discrepant stories in sound as we turn towards deep zones of engagement, to hear the oral histories of Indigenous nations and scholars and communities to attend to this land, this ravine and its resonances. This is our obligation of acoustic attendance: to decentre and disrupt the white and settled subject.

This is necessary.

The material world has a reactive power. While we construct and perceive our world through our own paradigms, material reacts against our abstractions, shattering them (Haeden Stewart, personal communication, 19 September 2013). Listening under the bridge, we understand noise as material. It disrupts our boundaries. It reveals our relations. In sound, (in) the (sonic) shock of the materiality of noise, maybe transformations can take place, points of connection can form, rifts can mend, and new relations can be made.

Can we hear how we are related? As we experience the intense materiality of our relations, can we also fully experience the intimacy of our proximity? Can we labour to understand the extent to which we are next to, engaged with, and integrated with the actual world around us?

Note 13 Resonance

In *The Coming Insurrection*, the French anarchist group The Invisible Committee reconfigures conventional Western European metaphors for revolution—they move away from disease and fire towards music:

> An insurrection is not like a plague or a forest fire—a linear process which spreads from place to place after an initial spark. It rather takes the shape of a music, whose focal points, though dispersed in time and space, succeed in imposing the rhythm of their own vibrations, always taking on more density. To the point that any return to normal is no longer desirable or even imaginable. (Invisible Committee 2009, 6)

The site under Mill Creek Bridge is composed of rhythms and vibrations of insurrection that are material and specific, that tell the stories of stream and ravine, of valley and river—stories that resist the simplistic white settler narratives of this place. Listening there, we begin to have some inkling of our "embedded ... diverse political and social implication[s]" (Bocking 2005, 3).

In the glossary of her book *Nationhood Interrupted: Revitalizing nêhiyaw Legal Systems*, Sylvia McAdam notes that her and her family's nêhiyaw name, Saysewahum (*sâh-sêwêham*), means "He Makes It (the earth) Vibrate" (McAdam 2015, 104). In the chapter titled "*manitow wiyinikêwina*: rebuilding a connection," Saysewahum (McAdam) writes,

A low hum could be heard through the universe, rhythmically broken by a consistent lull then the hum would repeat itself over and over again. No human memory could say when this hum began; only in the oral tradition of the *nêhiyaw* and *nakawê* people has it been told through the generations that it is foundational in the creation of mother earth. It is said when the Creator made *kikâwînaw askiy* (mother earth), the Creator took this same humming sound from the universe to create the heartbeat of mother earth. (37)[12]

To note that hum is to read with an ear turned and tuned to the hum of reciprocations and strangeness, the pulse of our obligations, the treaties that bind us, and then to listen in an attempt to repair that essential relationship.

Note 15 He[a]rd Hear Ear Herd

On 30 August 2013, Dwayne Donald (personal correspondence, 31 August 2013) sent me a link to a news story about the death of a large population of elk in New Mexico.

"Check these out."

Underneath the link with the news story was another that opened to a story told by a Blackfoot Elder named Kiitokiiaapii (2010) about the Elk Woman.

In the news clip, the story is composed, transposed through a camera lens, from a helicopter that hovers over the scattered and swollen bodies of the dead elk (Jensen 2013). Bears gather to eat the dead elk, and the newscaster reports the scene as a natural phenomenon, questioning how it will impact the hunting season.

In the Elk Woman story, a very old story told by the Blackfoot Elder Kiitokiiaapii, the same phenomenon has occurred. Somewhere near Yellowstone, a large number of elk have died mysteriously. Only Elk Woman, her mate, and a number of young elk are still alive. Elk Woman must follow a strict set of protocols, acting alone and making great sacrifices, to save the young elk. Ryan Heavy Head records and films Kiitokiiaapii telling the story; Kiitokiiaapii sits, looking into the camera. It is a very long story, based in a world view that reflects a dense network of complex and interdependent relations (ethical as well as physical). In the story, all the animals, including the humans, are involved, and there are precise actions that must be taken for the lost balance to be regained. The Elk Woman labours in her efforts to follow these precise actions, and the young elk are saved.

Watching Kiitokiiaapii tell the story, I am reminded of Voegelin (2010, xii): "Seeing always happens in a meta-position, away from the seen, however close, and this distance enables a detachment and objectivity that presents itself as truth ... hearing does not offer a meta-position; there is no place where I am not simultaneously with the heard." After listening to the Elk Woman story, I read Voegelin and hear "herd" (here) in heard. There is no place where the I is not simultaneously with the herd. To speak, to listen, is to live, as LaBelle (2006) says, "beyond [the] individual mind" (xiii).

Later, Dwayne explains that the Blackfoot story of Elk Woman contains miyo-wahkohtôwin, a Cree concept of natural law that refers to the eco-logical network of relationships that we rely on to survive. It refers to the way humans live in relation to a broad set of kinship connections, including those with the plants and animals. The term miyo-wahkohtôwin also extends to our relations with rocks—to the grandfather rocks.

Note 16 miyo-wîcehtôwin

Under the bridge, these relations are present in the rocky dust, in the trees of the ravine. In their materiality, and their interrelations, they exceed notions of authenticity and fixity. In this here, in these relations, the herd constitutes elk, rock, plant, human. Not determined by a Western European taxonomy, these boundaries constitute nests, full of silences, and points of connection: nêhiyaw, settler, stone, goosefoot.

Saysewahum describes the complex extent of these relations in her account of the Treaty 6 negotiations. She emphasizes the importance of the women lawmakers, the okihcitâwiskwêwak, in honouring, maintaining, and securing these relations:

> During the treaty making process, colonization and genocide had already taken a toll on many *nêhiyaw* nations ... A ceremony was conducted by the women lawmakers for four days and four nights asking the *âtayôhkanak* (spirit keepers) what must be done. During this time the women prayed and some fasted, as is the custom. An understanding was made and was taken to the men ...
>
> Further, during the ceremony *âtâyohkanak* entered the lodge with the women. There were many who entered but five made a declaration. The first *âtayôhkanak* that came was *pîsim* (the sun). The sun told the women, "I will

bear witness to this exchange and I will stand by it for all time." The second and third *âtâyohkan* was the *nipiy* (water), but it was the male and the female *nipiy* that came in and they, too, stated, "We will bear witness to this exchange and we will stand by it for all time." The fourth *âtâyohkan* was the *wihkask* (sweet-grass); the grass told the women, "I too will bear witness to this exchange and I will stand by it for all time." The final *âtâyohkan* was the grandfather rock, who stated, "I too will bear witness to this exchange and I will stand by it for all time." The grandfather rock is the pipe used to seal the exchange in what is now considered a covenant. (McAdam 2015, 57)[13]

Here, listen to these stories. Hear; reconsider previously unheard of relations.

Donald explains that miyo-wâhkôhtowin and miyo-wîcêhtowin inform the treaty sensibility that existed prior to contact. These crucial concepts informed how Indigenous communities understood the treaty talks with the Crown, the discussions on how land would be shared between Indigenous communities and European settlers: "You cannot understand the spirit and intent of the treaties or what it means to be a treaty person unless you understand the treaty sensibilities that the people brought to those talks. miyo-wâhkôhtowin and miyo-wîcêhtowin are at the heart of those sensibilities" (Dwayne Donald, personal correspondence, 21 September 2013).

For Saysewahum, these extended relations are familial relations: "Family is not exclusive to blood kin or extended family; wâhkôhtowin includes adopted family" (McAdam 2015, 59). To be in a good treaty relationship is to listen to and to understand the vast and complex circumference of your familial obligations.

nêhiyaw Elder Bob Cardinal reiterates this sensibility. According to his teachings, Treaty 6 is based on the original agreements of reciprocity that were made and have existed since the beginning of time—agreements of reciprocation that were made between humans and animals, between humans and air, between humans and water, humans and plants, humans and rocks (personal communication, 17 October 2014). According to Elder Cardinal, this is the most important thing we can know when we begin to consider treaty—that is, that these original treaties are the basis for the survival of all life on this planet, and they lay at the heart of the treaty-making process for the nêhiyaw people. That is, all subsequent treaties between Indigenous nations and non-Indigenous nations are based on these original and sacred covenants formed by humans and their more-than-human relations.

Would attending acoustically to these familial points of connectivity—animal, plant, rock—allow us to locate and address our relationships and obligations to this land, to each other, to the treaties? Would it allow us to inhabit these sites of historical and contemporary kinships in ourselves, rather than inhabiting the human as a site of isolated self and separation? Rather than inhabiting Canada's normalized state of crisis and oppression, could we listen to the vast intersecting sonic compositions to which we are both bound and oblivious? Could we note our obligations to these relations at the limits of our worlds, even if we are not yet aware of the extents of these connections? And could these practices have real effect in the world, leading to mutual agreements based in respect, resulting in the return of unceded lands?

Note 17 Line of Flight

In *The Fragile Absolute*, Slavoj Žižek (2000) demonstrates a link between Marxism and Christianity, arguing for a shared capacity for revolution. In contrast, he defines pagan cosmology as a claustrophobic, closed system of dense relations and carefully established protocols (122). As Žižek explains, Jesus and his followers join together through Pauline love (agape) and are thus rent from the organic communities into which they are born. Pauline Christianity radically enables its followers to detach, to "unplug" (121)—"If anyone comes to me and does not hate his father and his mother, his wife and his children, his brothers and sisters—yes, even his own life—he cannot be my disciple" (120)[14]—and offers the possibility of a universal subject ("neither men, nor women, neither Jews nor Greeks") through total separation from one's original community, acting as the miraculous derailleur that throws off the balanced circuit (121).

Considering the toxic concepts of the authentic that have animated thinkers like Uexküll, the emancipatory logic of Žižek's argument is clear; but the idea of the universal subject creates its own havoc. Perhaps there is something else—a possibility located in Žižek's critique of the kind of community he refers to as pagan—that it offers no hope of change, no line of flight.[15] Perhaps this is partly the significance of the Elk Woman story: that there is no escape—that is, that what we have, that what we hear (here), is it, and that points of possibility or change won't happen in the act of fleeing or eluding our embedded relations but, rather, in the disappearance of the isolated universal self (endlessly distanced in the visual, vanishing plane) and in the dissolution of the static, authentic community and subject.

Maybe after we have collected ourselves in the shifting but materially specific heard (herd) of this here, as listeners, rematerializing as combinations of precise physical and historical relations (not organic but material), engaged in the complex and difficult process of honouring treaty, we might be capable of something else.

Note 18 Phantasmic Freedom

The French anarchist collective The Invisible Committee (2009) writes that "freedom isn't the act of shedding our attachments, but the practical capacity to work on them, to form or dissolve them ... The freedom to uproot oneself has always been a phantasmic freedom. We can't rid ourselves of what binds us without at the same time losing the very thing to which our forces should be applied" (20).

This understanding of freedom resonates; it is felt through the contours of the body, through the humming connective tissues of one's endless familial relations, composed of diverse, divergent communities. What Žižek defines as imprisonment, and The Invisible Committee describes as the only possibility of actual, material freedom, I think Saysewahum, Cardinal, Donald, and Venne understand as "all of our relations." That is, there is no place wherein we are not simultaneously with each other and linked in all our deep and even sometimes dire relations. These attachments animate the listener, bending her ear towards all that is.

Note 19: Reciprocal/Inventive

Sound creates "a reciprocal, inventive production" (Voegelin 2010, 5). It is indexical, intimate; it traces a relationship that is (wholly) material (Haeden Stewart, personal communication, 19 September 2013). In listening, we are in sound, and so entwined. The very matter of sound is its condition of possibility. Sound functions as the thing that allows us to experience where and how we are. The sound of the underbridge manifests both the underbridge and the decentred listening subject and the absolute conditions (shifting) of those relations.

At 82nd Avenue between 95A Street and 93 Street, under the bridge, the world shifts; dust streams and sleeps; wires hum; people sleep and huff in mud and thistle; others walk and jog to siren wails and coyote calls. Hear this. What histories may be revealed as our awareness of our relations accumulate.

Listening here. A morphic ear. Hear, from down below, from beneath the bridge's promise, the underbridge: air drifts, voice flows, traffic runs, water drops, and warm steam hisses from the sewage grates. A dry leaf rattles in this high wind; that magpie calls. Everything matters. Everything counts and hums. Sound marks the presence of the complex and specific historical (bodily) relations of communities, of families, and our obligations, contiguous and infinite. Obligations based in ancient oral, legal, and ethical agreements. And maybe the underbridge desires its listener—and maybe we are inhabited, willed, drawn by this desire, its familiarity, compelled by its strangeness, oblivious and attentive. Our ears hear strange and estranging elements in a composition of a vast and dense discordant musicality, a resonance, a hum that disperses through earth, through bodies in time and space, that voices the materiality of time and space, and that voices our responsibilities to those bodies and that breathes breath out and into those stories that bind us.

And in those compositions, maybe there are possibilities for being differently in the world, for listening in uncertainty, in doubt, in the silence, moving towards something unclear, imbricated, and unknown. Not an "authentic symphony," but a clamour—a sometimes terrible but also beautiful dissonance, resonant, and insurgent.

Compositional Notes from the Underbridge and Listening Exercises
Jacquie Leggatt

On many occasions, between December 2011 and May 2012, Christine Stewart, Graeme Comyn, and I made recordings of the Mill Creek Underbridge. We aimed to capture a range of sound materials at different times of day and night. The resulting recordings include the sounds of joggers, dogs, children playing, snippets of conversation, wind, bridge sounds, many birds, and the ubiquitous traffic.

As I worked with the recordings as a composer, issues arose around combining and compiling these sounds. Was I making music? Was I trying to represent a "true" sound-image of the underbridge? Should I try to erase the sounds made by the person recording, or integrate them into the soundscape? What constituted a worthy recording, and what was simply detritus? As Christine notes above, previous approaches to depicting the soundscape seemed problematic and limited. Sound ecologist R. Murray Schafer's distinctions between "lo-fi" and "hi-fi" sounds reflect his view that noise is disturbing and needs to be reduced. Hildegard Westerkamp's (2013) intense subjectivity resulted in compositions that are as much about the person recording as about the sounds recorded. Brandon LaBelle's (2010a) research published in *Acoustic Territories*, like that of many current sound artists, focuses entirely on urban sound.

In working with the Mill Creek recordings, I was immediately aware of how the sounds, removed from their visual materiality, could be so intensely experienced, regardless of whether they represented nature, noise, beauty, animals, or humans. Each sound took on its own musical characteristics: suddenly, traffic sounded like wind, bridges like traffic, and children became birds. When I stopped naming and judging sounds, each one became its own rich and vivid site of resonance, and the intersections between these sites became clearer, resulting in an intense musical experience. It was in not trying to compose the sounds together, reduce noise, or create a narrative experience that I encountered and presented the "audibility" of the Mill Creek Underbridge.

Two projects have been realized with the recordings; they are archives and aesthetic gatherings, aesthetic perceptions of audibilities that resonate with the listening body, and that place the listening body. The first is a three-minute compilation of recorded sounds, which was played in Dettah during the Activating the Heart Workshop in June 2012. In this piece, contrasting recordings from day and night were looped and spliced together so that recordings from a wide range of times could be experienced simultaneously.

The second project is The Mill Creek Quilt. In this work, forty-five-second chunks of sound files are placed side by side or are overlapped to create a kind of aural fabric. The individual sections are available on SoundCloud, and we invite you to create your own Mill Creek Quilt with these sections.

On Listening

When we don't try to filter out what we consider unwanted sound, or insist on naming (and thereby dismissing) sounds, we are participating in an acute listening practice, extending our awareness, locating ourselves in the present.

Sound occurs among bodies (we hear; we overhear); sound generates listeners. Sound fully occupies space and other ears. Listening is a way of participating.

When someone speaks to us, we hear our own voice—not as others hear us, but resonating through the chambers of our skull.

How are places sensed? Steven Feld (1996, 91) describes a reciprocal relationship; as place is sensed, so are senses placed. His term "acoustemology" includes the local conditions of hearing, knowledge, and the cultural imagination.

Sound is never just sound. How can listening be used to consider history, language, water, earth, space, and justice?

We sought a practice of listening, an attentiveness to all sound, so that the listener is present to another world, so that the listener is present to its presence, alert to points of relation, for points of connection, and for the possibility of relations in this musicality.

By listening paratactically, we attempt to listen to the musicality that occurs as multiple worlds intersect.

Are you listening?

In our research practice, we become both reader and listener. We listen for the interplay of the universe. We listen to possible futures. We listen under the bridge for a past, for a present, for the land, and for this treaty. We invite you to also become both reader and listener.

Below, I have added two listening exercises that I have adapted from Pauline Oliveros (2005).

1 Exclusive Listening

According to Pauline Oliveros (2005), exclusive listening requires that you focus your attention on a single sound or group of sounds. Most of our listening is exclusive.

Take two minutes.

Listen to the sound of your breathing.

Can you hear your heart beat?

2 Inclusive Listening

For Oliveros (2005), inclusive listening is impartial and open; it seeks to encompass the entire soundscape.

Take two minutes. For a few moments, concentrate on the sound of your breath.

Then, consciously open up your awareness to all sounds—don't name them or identify them as beautiful or noisy.

Just listen.

Notes

1 The photographs for this phase of the project were taken primarily by Les Danyluk. Other photos were taken by John Houseman and me.

2 Agamben (2004, 43) notes that in 1928, Uexküll wrote a preface to Houston Chamberlain's *Die Grundlagen des neunzehnten Jahrhunderts*.

3 Agamben (2004, 42) links Uexküll's biology to the works of Paul Vidal de la Blache, Friedrich Ratzel, and Martin Heidegger.

4 The root *audh-* 'to perceive' is also linked to audience—an assembly of listeners. *Online Etymology Dictionary*, s.v. "audience (n.)," accessed 9 June 2017, http://www.etymonline.com/index.php?term=audience.

5 *Chenopodium urbicum*, or upright goosefoot, is both a weed and dinner, from the Amaranthaceae family, related to quinoa, beets, chard, and purslane. It has been cultivated and eaten in North and South America for thousands of years and grows all over Edmonton.

6 "Debris fields" is Les Danyluk's term for the swaths of debris that can be found under the bridge.

7 The *Edmonton Sun* states that "kâhasinîskâk" is the original nêhiyaw name of the Mill Creek Ravine (Lazzarino 2013).

8 Lewis Cardinal (personal correspondence, 17 November 2013) told me that it is believed that the migrating buffalo used the Mill Creek Ravine as an approach to crossing the North Saskatchewan, later heading back up onto the plains.

9 "[The] Overlanders, gold-seekers on their way to the Cariboo Gold Rush of the 1860s, crossed the ravine. As a member of the group later recalled, after two months on the road trip from Winnipeg, the 200 or so gold-seekers arrived at a particularly steep creek running into the river valley. The travellers had to cut a path through the dense growth of trees and

brush, then use ropes to lower each wagon one at a time and to pull each one up the far bank. The ravine made for hard work. But a few hundred meters farther on, they looked down on the river flats—and on Fort Edmonton on the opposite bank of the river. They had arrived in 'civilization'" (Monto 2013).

10 *Oxford English Dictionary*, s.v. "obsecrate, v.," accessed 25 November 2013, http://www.oed.com/view/Entry/129851.

11 Delgamuukw v. British Columbia [1997] 3 S.C.R. 1010 (Can.), accessed 20 November 2014, https://scc-csc.lexum.com/scc-csc/scc-csc/en/item/1569/index.do.

12 According to McAdam, this story is from her father, Francis McAdam Saysewahum, Saskatoon, Saskatchewan, 11 October 2014. See McAdam (2015, 107n2).

13 McAdam notes that this story came from an interview she conducted with Juliette McAdam (Saysewahum), 5 May 2010, Big River Reserve. See McAdam (2015, 111n99).

14 Clint Burnham and I write about this in the "21st-Century Poetics" special edition of *Canadian Literature* (Burnham and Stewart 2011).

15 This notion of "the unplugged" is important to Žižek because it bears the possibility of change. It also has resonance for me because it shares something with avant-garde poetics, in that the avant-garde often eschews the so-called personal in favour of language itself, universally speaking, confessing itself to itself.

CHAPTER THREE

Re-valuing Code-Switching: Lessons from Kaska Narrative Performances

Patrick Moore

Introduction

When addressing bilingual audiences, many Kaska storytellers code-switch between Kaska and English, a feature that Kaskas generally appreciate but many English speakers find objectionable. In this chapter I argue that the linguistic sophistication necessary for code-switching, as well as the creative ways that storytellers use changes between languages to enhance their stories, point to a need to re-value dual-language stories.

I came to fieldwork and language teaching with Yukon Kaskas from similar work with the Dene Tha in northwestern Alberta. The Kaska language and Dene Dháh (also called Alberta Slavey), the language spoken by the Dene Tha, are closely related, but the two regions have contrasting histories that have affected the use of the local languages (see, e.g., Moore 2007). The Alaska Highway and the Canol Road were constructed through Kaska territory in 1942, while the Dene Tha remained somewhat isolated from the resource-extraction economy and from governmental institutions until roads were constructed in their region in the mid-1960s. When I was living in the Dene Tha community of Chateh in the late 1970s and early 1980s, children spoke Dene Dháh as their first language, and there were many well-known storytellers. In contrast, in 1985, when I moved to Ross River, Yukon, the children there spoke English as their first language and most adults spoke English when non-Kaskas were present.

I had recorded many stories in Dene Dháh in the Dene Tha communities of Chateh and Meander River, Alberta, and I was interested in recording

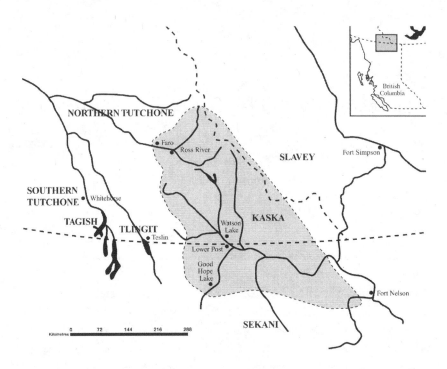

FIGURE 3.1   Map of Kaska Traditional Territory. Credit: Patrick Moore

Kaska stories for use with school programs, but when I visited Kaska Elders, they were reluctant to tell stories in the language. This began to change when language teacher Grady Sterriah and I visited Kaska Elder Maudie Dick one evening at her daughter Mary Dick's home. Dick and Sterriah both explained to her that I wanted to record her telling stories, and when she asked who I was, I told her in Kaska, "*Eskūkānī lēst'ē*" ('I'm a whiteman'). Maudie Dick was unable to see, and she apparently thought it unlikely that any white person would be speaking Kaska, so she told me, "*Gūnts'ít*, Carmacks *gūts'įh s̨ą dene lēnt'ē.*" ('You're lying, you must be someone from Carmacks'). She knew that I wasn't fluent in Kaska, and speculated that I must be from the neighboring community of Carmacks, Yukon, where the older indigenous members of the community spoke Northern Tutchone, and often learned Kaska from relatives and friends. She readily told us several stories in Kaska, which I recorded, including her account of how the diminutive culture hero Dzǫhdīē' used the knowledge revealed to him in his dreams to kill a giant worm (an excerpt from her account appears at the end of this chapter). Maudie Dick's preferred language was Kaska, and in her story she used a relatively small number of isolated English expressions, including *two, three, that girl, slough, some kind, little bit, any kind, Frances Lake, ground,* and *game.* It could be argued that these expressions constituted a limited set of unassimilated loanwords, rather than code-switching, since her fluency in English was limited.

Many people in Ross River later told me that Kaska Elder John Dickson was an excellent storyteller, and when I visited Watson Lake, Yukon, I went with Kaska language instructor Ann Mercier to see him at his home in nearby Upper Liard. He was indeed an impressive storyteller, and he recorded several stories during our first visit, including "The Girl Who Lived with Salmon," which appears at the end of this chapter. Unlike Maudie Dick, however, when his audience included bilingual Kaskas such as Mercier, he preferred to code-switch between Kaska and English throughout his performance. Since I wanted to document stories told in Kaska, whenever he used English I prompted him to use Kaska by telling him "*Dene k'éh zedlé*" ('Kaska way only') and by translating his English terms and sentences back into Kaska as he spoke. John Dickson was clearly used to telling stories by using both languages, however, so I soon abandoned my attempts to pressure him into using Kaska exclusively, and my ability to prompt him with Kaska translations may have strengthened his conviction that his dual-language performance was as appropriate for me as for Mercier.

As I worked with other Kaska Elders during the fifteen years that I lived in Yukon, many became comfortable telling stories and being recorded. Translation services were often provided for meetings, which made Elders even more comfortable using their first language, since they knew that they would be understood even when their audience included many people who didn't understand Kaska. With funding from Aboriginal Language Services Yukon, the Yukon Kaska First Nations and the Kaska Tribal Council also held language workshops and storytelling gatherings at which most of the audience was fluent in Kaska, which further encouraged the use of the language. While there was some overlap in the extent to which male and female storytellers code-switched between Kaska and English, male storytellers almost invariably code-switched more than female storytellers of a similar age, reflecting the gendered nature of social interactions between Kaskas and Euro-Canadians in the period before World War II.

Code-Switching, Personal Histories, and Evolving Language Ideologies

The dramatic differences in the extent of code-switching to English between Maudie Dick's and John Dickson's stories reflect their divergent personal histories as well as wider gender dynamics among Kaskas in the period before World War II. While the twenty Kaska storytellers I recorded for the *Dene Gudeji* collection (Kaska Tribal Council 1999) used varying amounts of code-switching, male storytellers used significantly more English than their female peers. John Dickson was older than Maudie Dick, but he used English extensively, while she did not. The two stories I have included here are representative of their respective styles when addressing bilingual audiences. Kaska men had more opportunities than women to learn English in the pre-war period because a fortunate few were able to secure employment with Euro-Canadians as special constables, guides, or labourers. Kaska men also took on prominent roles in dealing with local fur traders or travelling to distant trading posts to seek higher prices for their furs. The pattern of men engaged in wage labour gaining prestige in their community and fluency in the national language(s) parallels dynamics elsewhere in the world, as revealingly documented by Don Kulick (1992) for the village of Gapun in New Guinea, where the prestige of men employed in wage labour led in turn to valuing of the national language, Tok Pisin, which these men had acquired in the course of their work.

John Dickson was born at Mink Creek, near Kǫ́ą̄ Gūse'ānī (Pelly Banks), Yukon, to Ekétsī'éts and Bill Dickson. As a young man, John Dickson worked as a guide for Royal Northwest Mounted Police (RNWMP) Sergeant Claude Tidd, who was also an amateur photographer and whose photographs include images of John Dickson and his family.

Dickson was one of the only Kaskas to hold a regular paid position in the early 1920s. The other indigenous people employed in Ross River, the postman Bill Atkinson and the Anglican minister John Martin, were Métis and Gwich'in respectively and had acquired fluency in English prior to coming to Ross River. Other Kaska men in this period found irregular work as boatmen, guides, or woodcutters, but they primarily supported themselves and their families by hunting and trapping. John Dickson also hunted and trapped, and because of his leading position in the community and his ability to speak English he was selected as the leader of one of the two large group traplines

Figure 3.2   John Dickson, circa 1925.

Photograph by Sergeant Claude Tidd, Claude and
Mary Tidd Fonds, YA 7115. Used by permission of
the Yukon Archives

assigned uniquely to Yukon Kaskas. To assist them with their winter patrols, hauling wood and water, and other chores, the RNWMP regularly employed indigenous guides and special constables, such as Dickson, from the communities in which they worked.

John Dickson worked closely with Sergeant Tidd, and the two became good friends. In Ross River, Tidd had been dating an indigenous woman, Dehsele, widowed when her previous husband, a white man, had died at Fort Norman. When Tidd met a nurse in Fort Yukon, Mary Ryder, who would soon become his wife, he encouraged Dickson to start dating Dehsele, whom John Dickson subsequently married. Since Claude and Mary Tidd didn't speak Kaska, John Dickson gained considerable fluency in English while working for them, often translating for them and the many Kaska of the time who didn't speak English. Dickson accompanied Tidd on patrols, cooking their meals and performing other chores. He commented that Tidd, a thin and active man, was always hungry. The prominence that Dickson gained from his work as an indigenous guide for the RNWMP, and his fluency in English, facilitated his interaction with other non-Kaskas who came to the Ross River area, further enhancing his standing. He knew most of the trappers and gold miners who came to the Ross River and Pelly Banks regions after the Klondike gold rush.

Maudie Dick was born into a prominent Kaska family at Łūge Lě' (Weasel Lake) near Ross River. Her mother was Négūlēmā, Louise Dease, whose brother, Albert Dease, became a Kaska leader in the Dease Lake region and the main Kaska informant for James Teit (1917). Maudie Dick's father was Pelly Smith, and she had many brothers and sisters, including Dehsele and Neso Dickson (John Dickson's wives), Sadie Jules, Jim Smith, and others.

Maudie and her husband, George Dick, travelled widely within Kaska territory in southeastern Yukon during their lives together, hunting and trapping while living at Tū Désdés Tūé (Pelly Lakes), Kǫ́ą Gūse'ānī (Pelly Banks), Tehkêdení'ā Mené' (Sheldon Lake), Eghá' Dédā'ólī, Tū Łídlīnī (Ross River), and Upper Liard. In the period before World War II there were no wage-labour jobs for Kaska women, and they focused on subsistence activities and child care. Even after Maudie and George Dick moved to Upper Liard after the war to be closer to their youngest children, who were attending the nearby Lower Post Indian Residential School, they continued to use Kaska with their children when they were at home, and, despite the school's policies prohibiting the use of indigenous languages, all their children remained fluent in the language. The language ideologies and practices of most Kaska women in the period before World War II were apparently modelled on those of other fluent speakers, especially other Kaska women. They had relatively few occasions to use English prior to the massive social changes that accompanied the construction of the Canol Road and Pipeline and the Alaska Highway through Kaska territory in 1942. The limited use of English in the stories of Kaska women, as compared to those of Kaska men of the same generation, reflects gender differences in the pre-war period in employment, family roles, and language practices.

Creative Aspects of Dual-Language Narrative Performances

Telling a story in two languages requires knowledge of two, often contrasting, grammatical structures. For languages that are as different as Kaska and English, it is easier to switch between sentences than it is to switch within a sentence. Kaska sentences most commonly have the word order subject–object–verb (sov), as in *Essǫ tūzel ētsét.* ('grandmother soup ate'), while English sentences commonly have the word order subject–verb–object (svo), as in *Grandmother ate the soup*. The Kaska language also has extremely complex verbs that encompass many of the details of complete sentences. John Dickson and other Kaska storytellers who use code-switching more commonly switch between sentences (inter-sentential switches) rather than within a sentence (intra-sentential switches), and they often use a single language for a stretch of sentences. John Gumperz (1982) and others have reported this same preference for inter-sentential over intra-sentential code-switching for other languages. While Kaska storytellers use more inter-sentential code-switching, they also make fairly extensive use of intra-sentential switches. This form of code-switching has been the subject of extensive linguistic study, since using two languages within a single sentence poses particular challenges. Taking account of intra-sentential code-switching is also especially important for considering the creative aspects of dual-language performances, since it points to the artistry of speakers in combining both languages within a sentence. Carol Myers-Scotton (1997, 2004) has argued that code-switching is universally structured in terms of relations between matrix and embedded languages, a claim that has provoked debate (MacSwan 2005). Myers-Scotton contends that in code-switching it is possible to identify a matrix language that supplies "system morphemes," prototypically function words and inflectional affixes, while the content of the embedded language is restricted to "content morphemes," mostly nouns and verbs.

Code-switching Kaska storytellers such as John Dickson make use of two main strategies to satisfy the grammars of both Kaska and English while conveying key narrative cues, and their dual language use doesn't appear to be constrained by Myers-Scotton's proposed universals. Storytellers often use key Kaska expressions with narrative functions at the beginning of the sentence regardless of whether the rest of the sentence is in Kaska, English, or both, and they often keep the components of sentences, including noun phrases, verb phrases, or embedded sentences, in a single language. In some cases storytellers also use intonational phrasing and pauses to demarcate components of sentences (indicated in the transcripts and translations below by line breaks), further highlighting the points in the sentence at which intra-sentential code-switches occur. In (1) below, the sentence starts with the term *iyéh* 'then,' which is used to sequence events and indicate changes of speakers or scenes, followed by a Kaska noun phrase, which functions as the subject of the sentence. The rest of the sentence is in English.[1]

1 (Describing the medicine man giving the Salmon Girl food after her restoration)

Īyéh dene, nédetēī, IV (58)
Then that man, the medicine man,

you give her something to eat.

In (2), where the matrix language appears to be English (English predominates in this section), only *īyéh* 'then' and the demonstrative pronoun *didī* 'this' are in Kaska. Note that *īyéh* is a function word, and that this and many other examples from Kaska stories violate Myers-Scotton's proposed intrasentential code-switching constraints, that such switches will affect only content words, particularly nouns. Storytellers likely used Kaska for expressions with important narrative functions because they were more fluent in Kaska than in English and because the people they learned the stories from also used these terms in their stories.

2 (Describing her mother trying to cut the salmon [girl's] head)
Īyéh didī **last one**   II (13)
Then this last one

she take, cut its head.

Never cut,

Example (3) below starts with the Kaska expression *Ī lā sa'ă* 'long ago,' which has a temporal framing function in narratives. It then switches to an English sentence that has a Kaska noun phrase as the object, before continuing with a conjoined Kaska sentence, which specifies the identity of the subjects for both the English and Kaska sentences.

3 (Summary of the children's transgression)
Ī lā sa'ă' **they got a ługe** zǫ̀ze yéh ts'ídāne kenehtąh.   IV (72)
A long time ago children got a small fish and played around with it.

English speakers tend to devalue both extensive code-switching and the non-standard English of indigenous Elders. Analysis of the complex code-switching of storytellers such as John Dickson, however, reveals that speakers have extensive understanding of the basic components of both languages and creatively use the grammatical structure and narrative resources of both languages in their performances. Other studies of code-switching in Dene languages, such as Jeanette Wiens' (2014) study of Dene Sųłiné dual language use, have identified similar sophistication in the ways speakers satisfy the grammatical requirements of both languages while code-switching within sentences.

Although John Dickson was clearly more fluent in Kaska than in English (his Kaska is completely grammatical, while his English usage reflects the influence of Kaska conceptual categories and his experiences of learning English as a second language), he was able to use English not only as an emblem of prestige but also for dramatic effect. Often his narrative uses aligned with and enhanced established Kaska narrative techniques that undoubtedly predate the use of English. For example, Kaska storytellers often repeat key terms or phrases for emphasis, as in the following examples from "The Girl Who Lived with Salmon":

4 (Describing how her mother cried when her daughter disappeared)
   Łą̄ mōmā etsey.   I (38)
   Her mother really cried.

   Mōmā etsey.
   Her mother cried.

5 (Describing how the Salmon Girl is taken from a fish trap along with other salmon)
   Shāl,   II (4)
   Fish trap,

   shāl
   fish trap

   łūge tégedeleh,
   they were taking out fish',

   łūge tégedeleh.
   they were taking out fish.

John Dickson used echo translations, repetitions that switch languages, such as (6) and (7) below, for much the same purpose. In these cases, a language switch in either direction serves to further highlight the emphasis conveyed by repetition.

6 (Describing the girl's disappearance)
She's gone. I (33)

Endúé ejá.
She's disappeared.

7 (Describing the swan feathers used to cover the Salmon Girl)
Ī feather, II (26)
Those feathers,

feathers,

that here swan

chosé,

megígela.
they put over it.

The emphasis conveyed by both regular repetitions and echo translations is further reinforced by making the repeated element a separate intonation or pause group, as above.

Another important narrative use of code-switching in Kaska stories is to reinforce changes of voice, assisting audiences in identifying who or what is speaking in any particular part of the story. In (8) below, the Salmon Girl's initial word after she is restored to human form is differentiated from the narrator's voice by a transition to Kaska:

8 (Describing the revival of the Salmon Girl)
Medicine man IV (28)

He give her a little water,

tū, some warm water.
water, some warm water.

He sign the cross before he give it.

"Aneī!" he call 'em.
"Mom!" he [she] called her.

He call 'em as soon as he swallow that water.

    Like John Dickson, the medicine man in his story speaks both Kaska and English. His appearance in the story is often marked by a description in English followed by a transition to Kaska, as below:

9 (Describing the medicine man determining what happened to the girl)
    Medicine man,   1 (43)

    one medicine man he make medicine.

Ejin,
He's singing,

ejin,
he's singing,

ejin.
he's singing.

"Didī ī ahtsedzī negīyedéhtīn."
"That which you eat [salmon] took her."

10 (Describing the medicine man telling people what to do with the returned Salmon Girl)
    Well, he holler here,   11 (20)
    medicine man he come.

Łâyāl.
He came.

"Ī lēt'ē.
"That's it.

Ī tū' kílīn,
That water flowing,

Nāsdį' yege nénahtė."
Bury it across there."

The extent and nature of code-switching may be adjusted to fit the age and gender of the characters. The medicine man code-switches, but the girl's mother uses only Kaska, perhaps reflecting the restricted use of English by most women of John Dickson's generation. The girl, however, being a member of the younger generation, code-switches extensively.

While Kaska storytellers have identified English translational equivalents for particularly useful Kaska narrative devices, they also have the option of simply code-switching to Kaska to use these expressions. For example, Kaska has many expressions that are used for imitating sounds, which are rendered as one or more repetitions and as direct speech (as such, they also indicate a change of voice).

11 (Describing the knife scraping the necklace on Salmon Girl's head)
She take cut its head.   11 (14)
She cut its head.

Never cut.

"Gā́s, gā́s, gā́s."
"Gā́s, gā́s, gā́s." [cutting sound]

Storytellers code-switch to English to augment Kaska narrative resources in novel ways, including code-switching to set off a meta-pragmatic commentary (in this case an explanation of the story), as in the example below.

Scholars of code-switching such as Peter Auer (1995) have identified similar meta-pragmatic uses of code-switching in other languages.

12 Shāl,
   Fish trap,

I (4)

   shāl,
   fish trap,

   łūge tégedeleh.
   they were taking out fish.

   That's why metá' elīn,
   ***That's how it happened** that the father of the girl,*

   łūge tésegīn,
   he packed fish up,

   ten.

In other cases, echo translations have the meta-pragmatic function of explaining the meaning of culturally salient or uncommon terms through reference to English.

13 (Describing the cross on a necklace that the girl was wearing when she disappeared)
   That watch chain két'ē
   Like that watch chain

I (20)

   you got here

   sendíyā
   a cross

   that cross.
   that cross.

Kaska storytellers also use code-switching to the English pronoun *you* as in 13 above to identify audience members with a particular character in the story. This is another innovative use of code-switching, and in many cases storytellers then use a series of English sentences to give an instruction-manual-style set of directions.

14 (Describing children playing with salmon fry in a slough by the river)
Ts'ídāne tū yéh łūge dáchō kāgenahtąh.   1 (6)
Children were playing with small fish about this big in the water.

You make it slough.

Conclusion

The extent of code-switching in Kaska narratives reflects storytellers' personal histories and their relationships to the region's historic indigenous and non-indigenous communities. Unfortunately, code-switching in stories has been undervalued, because most English speakers have been socialized to reject both non-standard forms of English and the use of other languages within English discourse. Even scholars working with indigenous languages often regard code-switching to English as a form of contamination and a precursor of language shift. Scholars prefer stories told either in indigenous languages or in English, and as a result, stories that include extensive code-switching are under-represented in published materials. Although many scholars of indigenous languages and narratives don't think of themselves as language purists, they often encourage storytellers to speak one language exclusively, exclude dual-language narratives from their work, or eliminate code-switching through editing as they prepare stories for publication. The creative use of dual languages by John Dickson and other Kaska storytellers argues for increased appreciation of code-switching in stories. If nothing else, code-switching between radically different languages such as Kaska and English, particularly intra-sentential code-switching, represents an intellectual achievement that is all the more impressive considering the variety of narrative purposes that it serves. While scholars of indigenous languages and contemporary indigenous language activists may see such code-switching as the first stage of language shift to English, the prominent Kaska men who first learned English and who code-switched in their narrative performances were not simply capitulating to pervasive economic and political forces. They deserve recognition for mastering new languages and for creatively using them to pass on indigenous cultural traditions while innovating new ways of effectively conveying their stories.

FIGURE 3.3   Maudie Dick, Ross River,
Yukon, 1986. Photo credit: Patrick Moore

Kaska Stories

Dzǫhdīé' Kills the Giant Worm (First Act)
Maudie Dick, Ross River, Yukon, 1986

1

Sa'ǎ gūjáí,
Long ago,

Dzǫhdīé' lēsį̄,
Dzǫhdīé', I say,

Dzǫhdīé'.
Dzǫhdīé'.

Wédé dene mets'į́' nāndíbā kéhdī.
People always fought with him, they say.

Detsų̄ yéh négedē.   5
They [Dzǫhdīé' and his uncles] lived with his grandmother.

Łą́ ts'ídāne ją̄ tsį́' edéhchō.
He was the size of a child.

Dzǫhdīé', kéhdī.
Dzǫhdīé', they say.

Medese me'éné négedéł.
His uncles lived beside him.

Metsǫ yédé déh me'éné négedéłí.
His grandmother and the others were living there.

Ī, "Estsǫ, nénséstīn," nededī'.   10
"Grandmother, I dreamed again." he told her repeatedly.

"Echâ etsīhhágé gólí ust'eī, yē kah nentē endīa?
"Grandson, even though you follow your mind, what did you dream?

Esdāł kūndich," yéhdī.
Tell me about it," she said to him.

Kّét'ē gólí nūgeneh'ǫ́.
Even so he wouldn't reveal it.

"Estsǫ,
"Grandmother,

Ī kّét'ē, kūstl'ese k'ّá' esdege enhtsǭh.   15
those like that, make shrubby cinquefoil² arrows for me.

Two nétē ūntsǫ́ t'é,'" yéhdī.
Make two of them then." He said to her.

Łāyenّásgháts.
She sharpened the end.

Łāyenّásghádzi.
She sharpened the end.

69

Īyéh,—Dégíhdī lą?
Then—What do they say then?

Ī īhtį́' dét'īn kéhdī lą.   20
They said it was a red willow bow.

Īhtį́' détin, kíhdī'.
He had a bow, they say.

"Didī Estsų kę́t'ē esdege enghą́s," dī.
"Grandmother, carve it like that for me," he said.

Kę́t'e k'ígeh li.
He packed it around then.

Łą́ īhtį́' medege gūtīe yenīla'.
She really made the bow well for him.

I kūstl'ese k'á' ī medege, ts'e'ą̄ yę́dé,   25
She made those shrubby cinquefoil arrows for him,

melą̄h medege gūlayedeslā.
the points were already made for him.

Sedā.
He sat down.

Sa'ǎ negūjá k'ī,
After a while,

"Estsų̄, nénséstīn," nededī.
"Grandmother, I dreamed again," he repeated.

Łūge mǎ dene nédéł géhdī.   30
People were living by the edge of a fish lake, they say.

Nǻsdı̌',
on the other side,

kų́t'ē,
like that,

Kandāgenehílī t'ä́t néngedéł,
they were laying trees for lean-tos, living inside that,

łūge kį́'.
depending on fish.

FIGURE 3.4   John Dickson, Frances Lake, Yukon, 1992. Photo credit: Patrick Moore

Gédéni Gēs Gāgáh Nédē
The Girl Who Lived with Salmon
John Dickson, Upper Liard, Yukon, 1986

1
Down there,

someplace,

Dawson I think,

this side someplace.[3]

You know that little kid?   5

Ts'ídāne tū yéh łūge dáchō kāgenehtąh.
Children were playing with small fish about this big in the water.

You make it slough.

That here salmon,

salmon little bigger now.

Dánegede'él.   10
They dammed it.

All that three,

four kids.

Ya,

two girls,

two boys.   15

I sǫ ts'ídāne 'áné gedésdētl.
It must have been that those children went back.

That one girl he's gone,

about that big.

He[4] got necklace,

that watch chain kᶔt'e,   20
like that watch chain,

you got here

sendíyā,
a cross,

that cross.[5]

Ya,

ī są   25
it must have been

mōmǎ endúh.
her mother was gone.

Gee,

mekah k'égedél gólí,
they went around [looking] for her [the girl], but

endúh.
she was gone.

Ī ts'ídāne,   30
Those children,

One—two boys,

łūge yéh tū yéh kenetąh dé'.
they played with fish in the water then.

She's gone.

Endúé ejá'.
She disappeared.

"Nedúé ejá',   35
"She disappeared,

łą́ mekah kídzīyis ghǫh endúé."
they really ran around, but for nothing."

éhdī.
he said.

Łą́ mōmā etsey.
Her mother really cried.

Momā etsey.
Her mother cried.

Metá',   40
Her father,

all over.

"Dlēze neyedéhtīn są̀t'ē."
"Grizzly bear must have taken her."

Medicine man,

one medicine man

he make medicine.   45

Ejin,
He's singing,

ejin,
singing,

ejin.
singing.

"Didī ī ahtsedzī negīyedéhtīn."
"This that you eat [salmon] took her."

"Dedī łūge zǫ́ze ejá'.
"She became this small fish.

Gēs ejá'.
She became a salmon.

Ahtsá gíyedéhtīn.
They took her far away.

Bōt yéh gedés'ētl.
They went with a boat.

Kūhīnī kūdoge łūge dēt'īnī gebōdé' gúlīn.
They seem like fish to us, but they have a boat.

Dá gedés'ētl.   55
They travelled far by boat.

"Dígūht'ā łá endúé?
What happened that she disappeared?

Łéndūjá gét'ē.
Maybe she will come back.

Shāl enehlē,
You all make a fish trap,

kúhdigé
there

gedege nēdedáhlede dé.'"   60
before summer comes again then."

"Ham,"
"Yes,"

gedī'.
they all said.

II

Kúhdigé ts'ídāne nedū́é yige,
Where the child disappeared there,

łą́ dene nístlōn łédeł.
lots of people came there.

Kolā gēs kolā łâbel.
The salmon were already arriving.

Shāl,
Fish trap,

shāl,   5
fish trap,

łūge tégedeleh,
they were taking out fish,

łūge tégedeleh.
they were taking out fish.

That's why metá' elīn,
That's how it happened that the father of the girl,

łūge tésegīn,
he packed fish up,

ten.   10

Iyéh meyéhłīgé' łūge ahgan,
His wife dried fish,

salmon.

Īyéh didī last one
Then this last one

she take, cut its head.

She cuts its head.   15

Never cut,

"Gą́s, gą́s, gą́s."
"Gą́s, gą́s, gą́s." [cutting sound]

Kūłīnī et'ą́s.
She was cutting something,

Chain!
the chain.

Well he holler here,   20

Medicine man he come.

Łâyāl.
He came.

"Ī lēt'ē.
"That's it.

Ī tū' kílīn,
That flowing water,

nāsdı̨' yige nénahtě."
you all bury it across there."

Ī feather,   25
Those feathers,

feathers,

that here swan

chosé',
feathers,

megígela'.[6]
they put over it.   30

"Dūlą́ náné dene dūdūyą́ dé'.
"People won't go across then.

Megą́nahtān wédé,
You all watch it continuously.

tāchą̄ nāgūdīgā' t'é'."
tomorrow then when it is starting to get light."

III
Gee,

mōmǎ'
her mother,

she didn't know what she was going to do.

Dūlą́ cut 'em.
They didn't cut it.

Wédé megą́nehtān.   5
He always watched it.

Ī chos digé dą́já dé'.
Those feathers happened to rise then.

That foam kájā' digé dét'īn t'é.
There was foam that went up and down like that then.

"You got to see 'em.

Just esdógedije dé',
Just you tell me then,

sinī.   10
me.

Dūlą́ mets'į́' dūdūyą́ dé',"
People are not to go across to it,"

that medicine man.

"Sinī sąhdī mets'į́' ną́né dūgūssāyī."
"Only me alone, I will go across."

Chos megígīla'.
They spread feathers over it [over the salmon].

Īdéh mōmǎ wḗdé ną́né megą́nehtān,   15
Her mother always watched across,

māma,
her mother,

metá' k'ī.
her father too.

That he come here, foam.

Next time like that,

"Ahē."   20
"[She breathed in and out]"

the people they saw it like that.

That salmon nåsdį' sedā.
That salmon was sitting across.

Gēs sedā' į̂.
The salmon was sitting there before.

"Késédahdí dé'," éhdī, that medicine man.
"Tell me about it then," he said, that medicine man.

Dahch'ah mets' į̂' mōmǎ' łegedáhtl'a.   25
Suddenly her mother ran to there.

"Unǎ́ chos kétléjí̇ digé."
"Over across feathers are rising [with breathing]."

"Ham, kolā, kolā łénādāl lēt'ē," éhdī.
"Finally she is coming back," he said.

IV
Īdé' mets'į̂' degedáhya'.
He [the medicine man] went across to her.

More ejá' digé,
It rose more,

ī,
those

feather,

chos digé kítlich,   5
feathers rose with breathing,

ahghắne dé'.
rhythmically then.

Mets'į̀' āyālī.
He went to her.

He sign the cross like that.

Mets'į̀ nísdā.
He sat facing her.

He sing.   10

"Aní nahgūdūssį̀!
"Come here, I'm telling you all."

Dēsgúh left side esgáné' kédēdíj dé',
"I am going to lift my left arm,

ī netúé' elīnī."
the one that was your daughter," [he said].

Ī metá' k'ī,
Her father too,

just two zedlé' come.   15
just two, only those come.

Ā sa'ă gūjáí kédēdíj kájá'.
After a long time he lifted up [his arm].

Gee, tseygedáhtl'a'.
They ran up crying.

"Dūlą́ ahtsey!"
"Don't cry, all of you!"

éhdī.
he [the medicine man] said.

Ts'ídāne digé dá́t'ē sedā,   20
A child was sitting like this,

little girl.

Dāmă, dāmă gá́nehtān.
She saw her mother.

Ī gēs endú́h.
That salmon was gone.

Kāchōde that here gēs.
The whole thing, that here salmon.

Dene elį̄, metú́é.́   25
She was a person, her daughter.

Ī necklace right there.
That necklace was right there.

Łąsį̄ dé dūłą́ kūgūdé.́
She wasn't able to talk.

Medicine man

he give her a little water,

tū, some warm water.   30
water, some warm water.

He sign the cross before he give it.

"Aneī!" he call 'em.
"Mom!" he [she] call 'em.

He call 'em as soon as he swallow that water.
She called out to her as soon as she swallowed that water.

83

"Etŭé'!
"Daughter!

Kolā ła̧sį̄ endŭé,   35
Then there was nothing,

dzetsey yéh,"
we cried about it,"

gedī.
they said.

Metá', "Eté'é'!" éhdī.
"Dad!" she said to her father.

"Didī entsíe lā.
"This is your grandfather.

Ī łénehtēl lēt'ē.   40
the one that made you come back then.

Ī doctor elīn."
That one is a doctor."

"Eskǫ́ā̧ gūts'į́,
"At my house,

nahkǫ́ā̧ guts'į́',
At your house,

łą̄ esdege dēhjit, Mom," éhdī.
it's really stinky for me, Mom," she [daughter] said.

"Didī dek'éh neshegetīn.   45
"They slept where they had slept before.

Dene yéh tsá łâssāl.
I went downstream with people.

Atsé́ łą́ dene nístlōn.
Downstream there were really lots of people.

Bōt yēh dzā'ólī lāt'ē.
We paddled with a boat.

Ī birch bark boat yéh come up.
They came up with that birch bark boat.

Gūhīnī gūdege fish elīn.   50
For us they are fish.

Someplace we stop,

We sit down,

Like that we go out again,"

éhdī.
she said.

Kolāhóné' dene all ye come.   55

Finally the people all came.

"Łą́ dene désjit," éhdī.
"People really smell," she said.

"You stink."

Īyéh dene, nédetē'ī,
Then that man, the medicine man,

he give her something to eat.

85

He got that necklace, he cut it,   60

that here she's got her neck like that.

He's got his hair like that.

He give her clothes.

Momǎ' he give her clothes.
Her mother, she gave her clothes.

Now she get up,   65

she talk,

"Don't you so far.
"Don't you play so far.

Your life that here gēs," éhdī.
Your life, that here salmon," she said.

Dā meghąh négétsey.
They cried for her continuously.

One week gūjá' kolā   70
After one week passed

dáchō ejá'.
she became that big.

Ī lā sa'ǎ' they got a ługe zǫ́ze yéh ts'ídāne kenehtąh.
A long time ago children got a small fish and played around with it.

"Ǎ́! Ǎ́! Łogí!" gedī'
"Ǎ́! Ǎ,' Don't!" they said.

That's a true story that one.

That's a true.   75

That grandpa he tell me.

"You got to have here your kid,

you've got kid,

tell them, 'Don't play that łūge zǫ́ze.'"
tell them, 'Don't play with small fish.'"

Anyone,   80

that little fish, grayling, just like that you know.
little fish, grayling like that.

Don't play.
Don't play.

"Dūłą́ meyéh kenahtah! Ahtsedzī lēt'ē."
"Don't play with it! That's what you all eat."

Notes

1 In this and subsequent transcriptions, roman text transcribes spoken Kaska; bold text transcribes spoken English; and italic text is the English translation of spoken Kaska. In examples 1–3, Roman text transcribes spoken Kaska, bold text transcribes spoken English, and italic text is the English translation of spoken Kaska. In examples 4–14, words are rendered in bold to identify the feature being illustrated.

2 A small bush with yellow flowers, *Potentila fruticosa.*

3 He indicates that the story took place somewhere upstream from Dawson City, Yukon.

4 Kaska, like other Dene languages, doesn't differentiate gender grammatically.

5 Dickson described the cross as being like a Christian cross that was made of stone. Dickson believed that many aspects of Christianity, including knowledge of a supreme God, the wearing of crosses, and crossing oneself when praying, all preceded contact with missionaries.

6 Swan down was used by medicine men for a variety of sacred uses.

SECTION TWO

storytelling
to share

CHAPTER FOUR

Art, Heart, and Health: Experiences from Northern British Columbia

Kendra Mitchell-Foster and Sarah de Leeuw

Introduction

In his Massey Lecture *The Truth about Stories: A Native Narrative,* Thomas King writes that "the truth about stories is that that's all we are" (King 2003, 2). King, a Cherokee-Scottish author, references in the same publication other Indigenous storytellers, including Jeannette Armstrong, who writes, "Through my language [through stories], I understand I am being spoken to, I am not the one speaking. The words are coming from many tongues and mouths of the Okanagan people and the land around them." Andrea Menard, a Métis singer/songwriter and storyteller, reminds us, "it's not the colour of a nation that holds a nation's pride. It's imagination. It's imagination inside." Leslie Silko, a Laguna storyteller, is more direct: "[stories] aren't just entertainment. Don't be fooled. They are all we have, you see, all we have to fight off illness and death. You don't have anything, if you don't have the stories" (Silko 1977, 2).

We are two non-Indigenous women for whom these powerful words of King, Menard, Armstrong, and Silko describe core values and ideas that drive our work. The work in this chapter is reflective—it is storied and deals with issues of health from the perspective of the heart. Working from this embodied "heart of health" is important, especially when working with First Nations communities in northern British Columbia, Canada, because complex issues always involve both the head and the heart. The words of King, Menard, Armstrong, and Silko remind us that so much of what is privileged, especially in non-Indigenous world views and ways of knowing and being, centres on the head. Centring on *the mind* conventionally brings a bias toward logic as opposed to feeling and a focus on analytic thought as opposed to emotion.

Our reflections and discussions in this chapter focus on ArtDays, a unique research and educational effort growing in northern British Columbia, where we both live and work. Kendra relocated with her family to Prince George, BC, in 2013 as part of an intentional realigning of a daily way of life with values like family, hospitality, community, and justice. "I wanted my kids to grow up in a place that would allow these values to be more visible, more accessible and where resilience and inventiveness is an ingrained part of living," she reflects. "Having grown up on a farm in the Interlake region of Manitoba, I was seeking my social and spiritual roots, roots which were unconsciously steeped in settler identity. This became apparent to me in two ways as I made my life in a place more aware of anti-Indigenous racism and anti-Indigenous structural violence: (i) the ingrained settler notion that rural/northern/ remote geographies are uncivilized and barren, and (ii) the role of settler institutions like health systems and churches in reproducing harm and maintaining everyday colonialism. This awakening, for me, was in part facilitated through my involvement in ArtDays and the time spent in relationship with First Nations Elders and people who welcomed us to participate in their communities. Sharing these times of creating and learning gently brought forward a stark challenge to assumptions I didn't know that I had; a dredging and examining of my own history and positionality had begun. Who do I think I am? Who am I in relation to others? Who am I, as a settler, to work to challenge and dismantle colonialism and anti-Indigenous structural violence in my everyday life? These answers are continually changing, and they are continually transforming me as an ally."

Sarah grew up in northern BC, sometimes in communities with populations of less than 300 people, first on Haida Gwaii and then in Terrace, where she completed high school. She has very early memories of standing on a beach beside world-renowned Haida artist Bill Reid during the launching of LooTass, a Haida war canoe paddled off the beach of Skidegate in 1986: "This moment," she says, "is seared in my memory, a moment of art intertwined with a statement of cultural strength." As a creative writer and long-time activist-oriented northerner who has worked with women's and feminist organizations for more than two decades, along with health organizations such as Planned Parenthood, Sarah has spent most of her life in northern places, combining creativity (the literary arts) with political action. Fundamentally, she has always been incensed by things that seem unfair, including the marginalization of certain peoples and places. "How do people work together, and on ourselves," Sarah often wonders, "to address the ongoing colonial violences that are so etched in especially northern geographies? I do think art—and our hearts—have an important role to play."

As two settler women who live and work in northern geographies, in "small" places, and who choose to invest our hearts, minds, and energies in these places *as home,* we know intimately that the descriptor *northern* conjures a number of ideas, images, and preconceived notions about landscapes, ways of living, and the character(istic)s of people who live and thrive in these geographies. Some of these images hold true and are borne out by the seasons of the land, the warm hospitality of the people, and the beauty of the wildlife. Other images are more problematic.

We have witnessed that some of these images perpetuate racism, marginalization, and health inequity, particularly for Indigenous people, families, and communities who have thrived in these lands since time immemorial. The Indigenous populations in this geography experience some of Canada's highest rates of mortality and morbidity (de Leeuw et al. 2012), exacerbated by the ongoing challenges facing rural and remote communities in recruiting and retaining health care professionals, which leads to a perpetual shortage of care providers. Northern BC is a unique geography: per capita, a high percentage of the population is First Nations (one of the highest in Canada), and it is also home to the first modern-day treaty in a province that remains mostly untreatied (de Leeuw et al. 2012). The First Nations Health Authority (FNHA) is making history here as the first example in Canada of federal and provincial governments' delegating health services to First Nations control. We are seeing, both in the health sector and in academia, an increasing awareness of the need to partner with Indigenous communities and professionals to co-create Indigenous-specific and culturally safe modalities of medical care, practice, education, and research. Indigenous health paradigms, including those that form the operational foundations of the FNHA, have always emphasized health as a holistic enterprise inclusive of body and soul, heart and mind. We have found, and continue to find, that First Nations communities in northern BC are interested in forming relationships with health researchers and undergraduate medical students that support sharing knowledge about well-being (or lack thereof) in a holistic, creative manner. From this place of common interest, and from years of intentional relationships, the ArtDays project was born.

Placing Health and Art: Communities in Relationship and the Geographies of ArtDays

The dream of ArtDays, like those associated with health–arts or medical humanities efforts more broadly (see, e.g., de Leeuw et al. 2017; Kumagai and Wear 2014; Bates, Bleakley, and Goodman 2014), is to build relationships in artful and creative ways and to extend medical/health humanities into what is increasingly being referred to as "cultural safety" and "cultural humility" (Baba 2013). In the case of ArtDays, it began with two communities coming together in relationship—the first a small First Nations community in northern BC, and the second a group of health researchers and undergraduate medical students open to the idea of learning in new and non-deficit-based ways about the health realities of Indigenous peoples. ArtDays flourishes through an evolving partnership between the Nak'azdli First Nations[1] Health Centre and the Health Arts Research Centre. Our aim and hope is that Art-Days develops and strengthens positive (non-deficit-based) health-focused understandings between undergraduate medical students, health researchers, and First Nations people in a small reserve community.

Positive and non-deficit-based approaches to understanding health are important to discussing, co-creating, and developing the role of creative arts and humanities in health care theory, education, and practice with Indigenous communities. As we suggested in the opening paragraph of this chapter, stories and narratives are important components in this co-creation. Narrative, or story, allows humans to truly understand each other. Stories reach into human relationships; this can increase the likelihood of safe and supportive interactions, including those around complex medical challenges, and may even increase the capacity to deepen diagnostics (Charon 2001; Arntfield et al. 2013). To share stories is to engage in a reciprocal, relational act between individuals and/or groups (Charon 2004, 2006). In the realm of health and wellness, however, our focus is not simply on getting patients to tell their stories to health care professionals. Instead, we understand stories—narratives—as multi-directional tools that allow health care professionals to critically reflect on their own practices by understanding events relationally, over time, and across different spaces. For the communities with whom we have relationships, and with whom we have shared stories and have learned through stories and storytelling, there are well-documented linkages between health and well-being, a connection with place, and a strengthening of cultural capacities and sovereignty (Bunch et al. 2011; Parkes et al. 2009; Gupta et al. 2013; Halperin 2010; Richmond and Ross 2009).

Nak'azdli First Nation is located on Necoslie Indian Reserve No. 1, and serves sixteen reserves totalling 1,458 ha with approximately 1,700 on- and off-reserve members. The back and side doors of the large Kwah Community Hall, where ArtDays took place on several occasions before moving beyond it, open onto an unpaved parking lot abutting the gravel main street of this small reserve. Crests of Beaver, Bear, Frog, and Caribou, from the hereditary and traditional clans of Nak'azdli, are painted on the walls of the hall. The hall is attached to the health centre, which is staffed almost exclusively by nurses and community health and home support workers; there is no permanent physician on the reserve. The health centre serves as a community kitchen, a place for local youth and others to access free condoms, a place for healing circles addressing intergenerational traumas associated with residential

FIGURE 4.1
The Nak'azdli Health Centre,
Nak'azdli First Nation

FIGURE 4.2   Kwah Hall, Nak'azdli First Nation, during ArtDays.

schools, a dietician's office dealing with disproportionately high rates of diabetes, and the central hub for the recently revitalized tradition of annual naming ceremonies, wherein new babies are announced to their Elders, hereditary chiefs, territory/land, and fellow community members. Not so far away from the hall and the health centre, a community children's camp makes its home on the shore at Stuart Lake during the summertime; framed with pine- and cottonwood-covered hills, the cool and clear water reflects wide-open sky. Adults and children camp in tents and prepare and share meals in the fresh air; canoes and kayaks, among other equipment, supplies, and toys, signal a rich community recreational and learning environment.

The Health Arts Research Centre (HARC) was conceived of and is led by de Leeuw within the Northern Medical Program (NMP) at the University of Northern British Columbia (UNBC), a distributed arm of the University of British Columbia's (UBC) Faculty of Medicine (FOM). UBC's FOM is the second largest in Canada, and the NMP is part of its unique effort to educate future medical professionals in an immersive place-specific way that expands cultural and geographic competency and sensitivity; this attracts medical students (the physicians of tomorrow) from all over the country. The express

FIGURE 4.3   A south-facing view of the University of Northern British Columbia campus in Prince George, where the Northern Medical Program is located.

Image provided by University of Northern British Columbia

purpose of the NMP at UNBC, located in BC's "northern capital" of Prince George (pop. <80,000), is to train future physicians equipped with unique skills and perspectives that will increase their likelihood of practising in rural, remote, and northern geographies. One of its aims is expanding undergraduate medical students' understanding of First Nations peoples' unique historic and contemporary realities, including persistent and profound health inequities.

Class and cohort sizes are smaller at the NMP than at UBC; medical students work, study, and learn in more intimate relationship, and have more frequent opportunities to build relationships and to share experiences with one another and with professors and instructors over the course of their academic, practical, and applied clinical training. Geographically, the location of the NMP brings medical students into a northern context, and, very importantly, faculty and staff make a concerted effort to actively provide opportunities that bring the students socially, culturally, and emotionally into a northern context. Connecting with communities, landscapes, and ecologies with past and contemporary histories, and with cultural richness and tensions, brings a much-needed holism (sometimes successfully, sometimes less so) to the teaching, learning, training, and practice settings that medical students live and learn in. In general, upon admission to the NMP, these future physicians have little lived experience with First Nations or Indigenous health issues, nor have they been immersed in experiential learning about Indigenous health as socio-culturally, spatially, and historically constituted. ArtDays provided an opportunity to begin experiential engagement with the strengths and challenges lived in a small northern rural First Nations community. Ultimately, ArtDays—and related projects—centred on bringing multiple communities together to form heartfelt and genuine relationships of care.

The basic premise of ArtDays is to provide opportunities for First Nations communities and undergraduate medical students (not as outside "experts" with goals of tobacco cessation or blood-sugar monitoring, but as people interested in forming lasting and respectful connections with the communities) to form relationships. We hope that these relationships, often anchored in story, will create greater levels of trust, collaboration, and productiveness. Indeed, evidence suggests that creative arts have untapped potential in addressing health inequalities lived especially by marginalized peoples, including Indigenous peoples (Raw et al. 2012); that experiential learning leads to greater understanding by medical students of topics that require creative, complex, and empathetic responses (Crampton et al. 2003; Chastonay et al. 2013); and that shared experiences in creative expression can transform conventional social boundaries and cultivate more inclusive relationships and social norms at both local and broader levels (Hall 2013).

We see ArtDays as a transformative–emancipatory platform that considers knowledge linked to the values, interests, and status of the people who generate, use, and interpret that knowledge. In essence, ArtDays blends philosophical assumptions and approaches in order to engage with "wicked problems" (Tashakkori and Teddlie 1998, 2003; Ulin, Robinson, and Tolley 2005; Creswell 2009) by integrating and combining disparate experiences and perspectives to consider "otherwise baffling" situations, such as the divide between the arts, the medical health sciences, and Indigenous knowledges and communities. We propose that arts-based methodologies can facilitate this integration without compromising the integrity or validity of disparate perspectives (Creswell 2009; Johnson and Onwuegbuzie 2004;

Johnson, Onwuegbuzie, and Turner 2007; Johnstone 2004; Tashakkori and Teddlie 2003; Ulin, Robinson, and Tolley 2005). ArtDays makes an effort to bring together qualitative aspects of the human experience (values, opinions, culture) with empirical knowledge (pathologies, disease risk metrics) (Creswell 2009; Mertens 2003; Tashakkori and Teddlie 2003). A concern with social justice forms the foundation of this transformative–emancipatory work, work in which we seek to change asymmetric power dynamics, social inequity, and marginalization of people or groups of people (Mertens 2003). A central assumption of transformative–emancipatory work links directly to cultural safety in care: people ought to have influence and power in decisions made about their own health, and over the ways in which services, supports, and care are planned, presented, and provided; special consideration ought to be given to populations, like Indigenous people in northern BC, that are systematically subject to pervasive social and political exclusion (Mertens 2003).

ArtDays: The Heart of Arts and Building Relationships

We co-created ArtDays events with Elders, community members, and community health practitioners in 2011, 2013, and 2014 in the Kwah Hall at Nak'azdli, in the Nak'azdli Health Centre, and on the shores of Stuart Lake. Relationship and trust-building efforts over the past seven years have produced fruitful research partnerships and generated invitations from the community asking the researchers and medical students of our research team to return. Endorsed by the elected chief,[2] ArtDays were co-sponsored by the Nak'azdli Health Centre and the NMP at UNBC. The days were co-facilitated and co-organized by staff from the Nak'azdli Health Centre (nurses and home support workers), undergraduate medical students and faculty in the NMP, and graduate students from UNBC's Community Health Science Program.

Because ArtDays is designed to explore the potential of artmaking and experiential learning through shared creative spaces to renew health and well-being in a community with many strengths, we consider it a wonderful fit for deep questioning in the community of Nak'azdli. We invited second-year medical students from the NMP to share in organizing, facilitating, and undertaking artmaking sessions; they also reflected on the experience of being invited into a shared creative space with the intent of challenging their own assumptions and deepening their understanding of participants in the geographical, cultural, and physical context of a remote northern BC reserve.

Creative expressions, including storytelling, visual arts, music, literary writing, collaging and crafts, mask making, and telling stories while sharing food were all central to the work of ArtDays. Since the majority of participants (First Nations community members, student learners, and researchers) have spoken about entering this creative space feeling self-conscious about "not being artists," activities such as non-directive "mark making" followed by storytelling about the resulting images (see Figure 4.4) created a space for expressing perspectives on health and well-being. In mark making, we create images with our eyes closed, working from a place of pure feeling; trust and relationship building become the entry point to discussing health using creative method/ologies. We sought to create an environment in which creative (and heartfelt) expression could dismantle the conventional power dynamics of interactions between community members and health care practitioners – in this case, Indigenous communities and medical students. These approaches to understanding health are important and particularly relevant to discussions about the role of creative arts and humanities in health care theory, education, and practice involving Indigenous communities. Our collective experience through ArtDays emphasizes this importance, as we were able to engage with Indigenous communities' well-documented linkages between health and well-being, connection with place, and strengthening of cultural capacities and sovereignty (Bunch et al. 2011; Parkes et al. 2009; Gupta et al. 2013; Halperin 2010; Richmond and Ross 2009).

"A woman came into Kwah hall looking for someone," recalls Kendra of the story Sarah told her.

Apparently she was looking quickly, appearing like she did not want to chat, interact or get involved with what was going on (ArtDays). She was a granddaughter, daughter, wife, and mother. As we invited her in to share food, create some art, share some stories and spend some time in community, she became interested and irritated at the same time. She had had a morning. A hot morning. The berries were good in the patch that her grandmother had always taken her to, there were a lot, they were ripe and they needed to all be picked before they went bad. It was a hot summer day, clear skies and bright sun shining, the picking was good early, but as the sun reached the peak of noon it was sweltering. She had been picking with some other women early, and they had finished what they wanted to do and had gone home. She had been picking by herself by the time the midday sun rolled to its zenith. She ate and drank as she told the story, when she had finished, someone at the table encouraged her to draw that sun. Draw that morning. As the image of the red-hot sun emerged her frustration gave way to other stories, chatting with others at the art table and laughter here and there. Just as abruptly as she arrived, she got up from her chair and went on her way out of the hall, leaving her image behind for the ArtDays collection.

This recollection conveys well the spirit of ArtDays. People arrive to famil-iar and comfortable places in their own community to find an opportunity to make art and engage with their own stories and the stories of others in authentic ways. Spontaneously sharing the details of their lives reveals more than just the goings-on in a community; community and family ties are revealed, and priorities, family legacies, knowledge passed down through generations, collective memories, landscapes and resources, familial and community culture, and the richness of interwoven micro-logics emerge

FIGURE 4.4   Seeing, feeling red: a sketched visual window into a day picking berries in the northern hot summer sun.

FIGURE 4.5
Artmaking at Stuart Lake.

as well. For community members, this can be a non-threatening and non-manufactured way of helping a medical practitioner, health researcher, or medical student learn about life in places that they have never been before (socially, culturally, geographically). For people invited into First Nations communities to work, live, and/or practise, it can be less intimidating to learn by listening and participating; it can be a low-barrier environment where challenging settler guilt, assumptions, and socially ingrained anti-Indigenous racism is safer, gentler, and supported.

Nine separate four- to eight-hour sessions were held in the summers of 2011, 2013, and 2014: five full days and one half-day held in Kwah Hall, one half-day with adults holding a children's camp at Stuart Lake, two walk-in all-ages artmaking sessions at the community health centre, and an Elders-specific art and craft session also held at the community health centre. Participants were recruited by word of mouth and event promotion through posters and other media. The ArtDays sessions asked participants to consider how they thought art influenced their own or their communities' health, and to choose a medium of artistic expression, including drawing, painting, sewing, weaving, dream-catcher making, sculpture-making, mixed media, music creation, and creative writing. ArtDays participants completed short surveys before participating, which addressed the links between creative self-expression and health and well-being. The ArtDays research team supported medical students to use self-reflection exercises to integrate their immersion education experiences (on-reserve artmaking sessions) and then engage with facilitated reflection. Health provider partners serving Indigenous communities also observed the learning processes and outcomes of the immersed medical students as part of a facilitated reflection exercise. As researchers, we undertook ethnographic observation, adding context to broaden the frame through which the research would explore participants' interactions and reflections on artmaking activities. Semi-structured telephone or in-person interviews during and/or following each ArtDays series also facilitated a deeper exploration of participants', students', and practitioners' perceptions of and opinions on the effects of creative arts on care relationships involving Indigenous people and their communities in northern BC.

Principles of empowerment and liberation lie at the core of the work we present in this chapter. Our research relationships reflect the belief that research should be community driven and aspirational; should focus on building local capacity, starting with existing strengths and ways of being; and should drive efforts toward emancipating communities and people from any oppressive or debilitating conditions in which they live (Israel et al. 2005; Minkler and Wallerstein 2003; Stringer 2007; Cornwall and Jewkes 1995; Minkler 2004, 2005). Communities include a diverse array of experiences and knowledges, and should be engaged as co-learners, co-researchers, and co-practitioners with equitable weight in directing, undertaking, and evaluating collaborative research (Cornwall and Jewkes 1995; Israel et al. 2005; Minkler 2000, 2005; Minkler and Wallerstein 2003; Stringer 2007; Wallerstein and Duran 2006). The explorations we have outlined above (using multiple-methods approaches), driven by the values described here, allowed us to identify themes relating to concepts of health and healing, and in particular, cultural safety.

Communities in Relationship with Place and Each Other: Towards Culturally Safe Engagements

Cultural safety in health care and health service delivery is more than eliminating racist anti-Indigenous sentiment from language, practice, and institutions; it encompasses a paradigmatic shift in ways of understanding relationship and relationality in care. Fully honouring and empowering Indigenous identities is integral to this shift, which requires affirming, rather than denying, all aspects of personhood in cultural, spiritual, personal, emotional, physical, and relational dimensions (Williams 1999; Ball 2008; Papps and Ramsden 1996; Smye and Browne 2002). Cultural safety also emphasizes recognizing and disrupting destructive inequitable power dynamics and hierarchies in care. The experience of ArtDays has shown our collaborative research team that arts-based methodologies can engage the complexities of cultural safety in relationships in non-threatening, strengths-based ways (Belfrage 2007; Smye and Browne 2002).

Indigenous-focused research must be built upon relationships of reciprocity and trust (CIHR, NSERC, and SSHRC 2010). Our ArtDays collaborative research, exploring the reach and validity of Indigenizing arts practices and creative or humanities-based method/ologies for researching health needs and perspectives of Indigenous peoples in northern BC, is no exception. Our work builds on more than five years of community-based research in which creative arts have strengthened relationships and provided a platform to address health realities for both Indigenous and non-Indigenous peoples in northern BC communities.

Cultivating a sensitive understanding about and respect for the places and geographies within which Indigenous ways of being, ways of knowing, and histories are rooted is key to practices of cultural safety. Remoteness is a characteristic often ascribed to First Nations and Indigenous communities in northern BC; in a wider (non-Indigenous) Canadian context, the label "remote" carries connotations of disconnection, lack of civilization or "wilderness," and being "in the middle of nowhere" (de Leeuw et al. 2012). These perspectives rely on colonial ideas about civilization, privilege urban-centric economic and social structures, and give rise to assumptions about the lives and behaviours of people, communities, and populations that live in rural and remote settings. Descriptions and understandings of community, in this sense, affect the depth and breadth of trust and connection within collaborative relationships, which, in turn, can determine the transformative potential of community-driven work (Eng et al. 2005; Wallerstein and Duran 2003).

Cultural safety includes honouring "remote" landscapes as fully known and inhabited by the lives and past lives of whole peoples and, despite the number of Indigenous peoples living in urban geographies today, as places in which Indigenous peoples have thrived and been healthy since time immemorial (Belfrage 2007). There is a rich diversity of experience, culture, and ways of living in these settings, requiring health service practitioners to intentionally and conscientiously include cultural safety as a central focus in education, training, and practice (Bourke et al. 2004). Remoteness is a lived reality and a determinant of health, but it also serves as a socio-geographical barrier to improving cultural safety in health care through improved medical education (Klopp and Nakanishi 2012), service delivery practice, and health promotion (Bourke et al. 2004). From this perspective, we believe that honouring the embeddedness of human nature, appreciating the strengths and diversity of communities and their ever-evolving social fabrics, includes taking the broadest possible view of how different people, groups, associations, and communities are connected to and affected by complex human health issues. Human beings, human families, and human communities are inextricably linked to the systems within which they live and thrive: social systems and connections with others, cultural systems and deeply rooted ways of being, spiritual connections to tangible and intangible elements of the universe, ecosystems and ecology, and political, economic, and historical systems (Eng et al. 2005; Forget 2001; Forget and Lebel 2001; Lebel 2003).

Stories and Relationships in Nak'azdli

The ArtDays project is sustained by our team's commitment to establishing and maintaining a culturally safe and respectful relationship with the Health Centre in Nak'azdli. It was transformative for students, researchers, and community participants alike to enter into a communal creative space in Nak'azdli to make art, to share creativity and creative expressions, to learn about cultural expression rooted in place, and to explore lived health inequities—with intent—in order to build relationships: one First Nations community participant noted that making art "takes your mind off life's struggles [and can] give a sense of self-worth," gently teaching student participants about the importance of a strong sense of self-worth for rural Indigenous peoples. As art was made throughout the day, other First Nations participants noted that "[a]s First Nations we use art [to] identify what community we come from" and that art helps people "to be able to express themselves in ways they normally can't." For their part, medical students took other, less didactic lessons away, for example:

> There are different reasons to do art. [We] must look at the intentions behind doing art: to win, to cope, to heal, to make money, for enjoyment and leisure. Making "good art" was not the goal of ArtDays; instead, it was to explore the role of art in aiding health and healing.

FIGURE 4.6   Art created by people participating in Nak'azdli ArtDays, exploring the relationship of health and places that make us feel healthy.

There is an overwhelming consensus in Nak'azdli that creative arts hold significant potential for documenting, understanding, and changing Indigenous peoples' health and ill-health experiences from a strengths-based perspective, and that research informed by and using creative arts methods may have therapeutic potential for participants. In 2013, twenty-four of twenty-seven ArtDays participants answered "yes" when asked if art had the potential to improve First Nations' health and well-being; there is broad agreement in Nak'azdli that art serves unique and specific functions for their communities in the context of health and healing. Some participants referred to the health-related challenge of passing on important intergenerational knowledge and stories:

> I truly believe that this [art production] is a good way for people [First Nations] to deal with issues such as residential schooling. [We need to] grieve.

> *

> [A]rt/creative expression can help them [younger people] learn about how to live and love one another. To respect Mother Earth and creatures that were created for Mankind. To know what respect really means. [It can help] to teach little ones know what love means.

Many participants spoke of art and creative expression as having healing abilities: the ability to bring people together, to provide a means to convey emotions and stories that are otherwise difficult to express, and to engage with traditional ways of developing and strengthening identity. This gathering and immersion in creative expression, and the relaxed discussion and chatter that participants engage in while creating, teaches newer generations and people unfamiliar with ways of being, ways of knowing, and ways of living in Nak'azdli about the rhythms of the community and the knowledge held by Elders. Participants and students reported experiencing stress relief, peacefulness, positive feelings, a sense of accomplishment, and self-confidence. Participants saw art production as a means of exploring and understanding health and ill-health holistically through "healing for mind, body and spirit!" and as a way to celebrate strengths and resiliencies:

> When I'm scraping moose hide, it's a form of meditation for me. It gives me time to think for myself and solve problems. When I pick berries, it's time for

meditation, peace, and tranquility. A time to reflect calmly. I can the berries. It gives you food. Connects me to the land.

*

Older people [must] find other forms of creativity because moose is getting endangered and supplies are dwindling. Art is all around good, physically and mentally. I feel very good if I finish a pair of moccasins.

*

I absolutely believe [that art can better health in First Nations communities]. It is doing it in our traditional ways. Yes, in an Aboriginal way. They are giving themselves therapy through their traditional identity such as carving, weaving ...

*

[A]rt is a freeing of the emotions and thoughts held within, whether good or bad. The release of them in a creative environment without limitations allows the body, mind, and soul to become free.

Exploring health and healing through creative and storied processes allowed participants to convey heartfelt, nuanced, and complex visions of well-being to one another and to facilitators, including medical students. These artistically crafted dialogues emphasized the importance of connectedness to health and imparted a holistic and dynamic conception of health and healing. Constructing these visions in a communal creative environment fostered a culturally safe atmosphere, supporting community participants and researchers in connecting, sharing ideas about health and healing in empowering ways, and gaining insights that more typical contexts of interaction would preclude.

The connections medical students made about cultural safety and the crucial link between place, health, and identity for First Nations community participants were of particular importance:

Working in the north, working with people that are strongly rooted to place as part of their identity, is totally contrasted to understanding [place] from [the perspective of a] Vancouverite—as everyone being from a different place and making their own space wherever they go.

*

Following the rhythms of a community with everyday realities like berry picking in the morning, however, demanded a new understanding of time, and the perceived importance of things like research projects. (Klopp and Nakanishi 2012)

*

I expected [children at the lakeshore camp] with a potentially different, lower level of discipline, because of my preconceptions of First Nations child-raising. With the information we are exposed to about residential schools, the stolen generations, and the dysfunction of families and parenting skills, I was expecting this to be manifest in these [children, in these ways].

One of the more significant findings of our research is that art and creative expression have a remarkable capacity for training future health care professionals in cultural safety (Polaschek 1998; Walker et al. 2009). Since anti-Indigenous racism is a determinant in First Nations people's access (or lack of access) to health care (Bourassa, McKay-McNabb, and Hampton 2005; Henry, Houston, and Mooney 2004; Marrone 2007; Browne and Varcoe 2006; Shahid, Finn, and Thompson 2009), strengthening physicians' and other health care professionals' understanding of and empathy toward the causes of the causes of Indigenous peoples' health statuses might well lead to better health care for First Nations (Browne, Smye, and Varcoe 2005; Polaschek 1998; Walker et al. 2009; Nguyen 2008; Kagawa-Singer and Kassim-Lakha 2003; Wear 2003). Through art and creative production, as opposed to a clinical encounter, ArtDays provided a starting point for future health practitioners to enter into discussions about culture, colonialism, the determinants of health, and the needs of First Nations (Klopp and Nakanishi 2012).

Medical education centred in urban universities and hospitals (where Indigenous people are under-represented among students, staff, and faculty) creates a learning environment that is culturally and socio-geographically removed from the lived realities of rural northern First Nations communities (Crampton et al. 2003; Dussault and Franceschini 2006; Murray et al. 2012). Students learn about Indigenous communities and their health through an academic, theoretical lens, without whole-person experiential learning; this fosters (often pathologizing) assumptions about First Nations people that affect clinical care and doctor–patient interactions at the individual level (Tang and Browne 2008). Medical students who participated in ArtDays identified and challenged their own assumptions about the health and well-being of Indigenous communities, families, and people. Furthermore, these students believe that their ArtDays experience will continue to have a positive impact on their current and future interactions with Indigenous people in a clinical setting. Using art and creative expression methods, as well as critical reflective writing, in a forum like ArtDays could begin to address the important gap between conventional training and the experiential knowledge needed to support culturally safe clinical and public health practice.

ArtDays provided a foundation for medical students to engage with First Nations communities, as well as with deep-seated issues of settler–Indigenous relationships and decolonizing practices of research and medical education. Medical students offered reflections that described assumptions and expectations about ways of being, based on their own experiences of community and family structure, social interactions and relationships, and health and healing in (mostly) non-Indigenous communities and environments. Conversation, interaction, observation, and engagement with community members from Nak'azdli helped the students identify personal development opportunities around cultural safety that would otherwise have been invisible, intimidating, overwhelming, or inaccessible through conventional medical education.

Different World Views Meeting in a Creative Space

Arts and creative expression are linked to cultural strength and well-being, particularly for Indigenous peoples, whose cultural identities and creative knowledges and practices were aggressively destabilized by colonial interventions across wide spans of time and space (Stewart et al. 2008; Currie et al. 2013; McIvor, Napoleon, and Dickie 2009; Zurba and Berkes 2014; Richmond and Ross 2009). These linkages go largely unrecognized in current Canadian medical practice. The discipline of medicine has deep positivist roots in western culture and practice, often with a colonial history, especially for First Nations in British Columbia (de Leeuw et al. 2012; Kelm 1998). Medical education pedagogy and paradigms, therefore, have entrenched modalities and beliefs around knowledge, the medical doctor as expert, power hierarchies, and understandings of health and well-being. The result is a pervasive culture in medicine, and in medical schools, of applying reductive and deductive logics to biomedical science models for illness-centric curative practices. In addition, medical schools are most often located at larger universities in urban centres, where discursive and material spaces are steeped in intense expectations of the highest productivity and achievement (Enns et al. 2001); it is within these human geographies that medical education unfolds, that future doctors are taught (de Leeuw, Parkes, and Thien 2014). Discomfort with emotions, emotionality, and personal expression often bleeds into the medical student experience, and time dedicated to exploring these aspects through education modules and assignments often frustrates students because they are not specifically learning biomedical science (de Leeuw et al. 2014). The role of emotion in medicine and medical training is relegated to peripheral skill sets, acquired somewhat haphazardly through experience and personal capacities rather than systematically honed through training, mentorship, and education underpinned by a holistic pedagogy. In sum, the heart is difficult to find and place within many medical and health relations, especially between Indigenous and non-Indigenous communities.

A wealth of research and published literature demonstrates strong links between Indigenous peoples' desire for holistic, emotive, health and the creative arts, broadly defined (Archibald 2008; Allard 2007; Canada Council for the Arts 2010). Indeed, as we have discussed elsewhere (Muirhead and de Leeuw 2012), given the long-standing understanding that medicine is both a science and an art (Vaccarella 2011), the creative arts (including storytelling, creative writing, dramatic and/or musical productions, photography, dance, and visual arts) offer ways to bridge the divides that currently exist between a health care system and research paradigm of predominantly non-Indigenous values, practices, and modes of care, on the one hand, and Indigenous world views and understandings of health, on the other. Exposure to traditional and modern forms of Indigenous art has the potential to stimulate interest in Indigenous culture and respect for the dynamic, resilient, and unique place Indigenous peoples hold in Canada, both within Indigenous communities and in health care practitioners and settings. The Royal Commission on Aboriginal Peoples (Canada, RCAP 1996) argues for mutual recognition of the value of cultural expressions and practices as a basis for improved relations between Indigenous and non-Indigenous peoples. Creative arts may thus open new spaces for medical and other health professional students to critically reflect on their practices and attitudes and to consider culturally safe and relevant modes of care with reference to Indigenous peoples (Klopp and Nakanishi 2012; de Leeuw et al. 2012).

Furthermore, as we have noted elsewhere (Muirhead and de Leeuw 2012), a key recommendation of BC's Provincial Health Officer's 2007 Annual Report, which focused on improving the health and well-being of Indigenous peoples in the province, was to "revive cultural and spiritual traditions to aid in the healing of community members" (British Columbia Provincial Health Officer 2009). Along with a growing body of research demonstrating that creative arts can improve health programs, practice, research, and teaching (Charon 2006; Cox et al. 2010; Willson 2006; Donohoe 2010; Fiske 1999), the arts may have a valuable role to play in health and socio-cultural (including spiritual) revitalization of Indigenous peoples. In her work with Cree people in northern Quebec, health practitioner Nadia Ferrara (2004) found that many of her patients struggled in traditional modes of health care involving verbal communication, yet felt much more comfortable addressing various health issues through art. Ferrara attributes success to the creative portion of art practice, in which people draw or paint (or perform) what they are thinking or feeling. In her experience with Cree people, talking about and verbalizing emotions creates a power hierarchy between health care provider and client, a power imbalance misaligned with the norms of Cree society, in which individuals are expected to maintain a level of autonomy and personal control that allows the collective to function efficiently (Ferrara 2004). In western/settler society, by contrast, these inequitable power relationships between providers and clients are accepted and often promoted. Using creative methods as communication and research tools in Indigenous health care settings may be effective in bridging divides between primarily non-Indigenous health care systems and providers, on the one hand, and Indigenous world views and understandings of health, on the other.

Growing Momentum and Continued Creativity

While connections between creative arts, medicine, and health are still embryonic in Canada, medical curricula elsewhere increasingly use concepts and tools from the humanities to advance students' and physicians' understanding of healing, pain, suffering, and therapeutic relationships and to encourage self-awareness, humanity, and professionalism (Cox et al. 2010;

Shapiro et al. 2009). The fields of narrative medicine hold particular promise, especially given the power of storytelling for Indigenous peoples (Archibald 2008). Concerned with both clinical practice and theories of care, narrative medicine is informed by concepts common in literary studies and the literary arts (Charon 2004, 2006) and moves away from a biomedical paradigm that frames human ailments primarily as problems that can and must be solved in clear and evidenced-based ways. Instead, narrative medicine works towards conceptualizing illness and wellness as experiential in nature, and thus as requiring patient narratives to be expressed, understood, and therapeutically addressed. Narratives capture our interest, encourage readers and viewers to look at the world in new ways, and often compel us to think along lines and about topics we could not have imagined prior to entering the story. Scholars of narrative medicine argue that these traits of narratives are precisely what make them potentially so valuable to medical theorists and clinicians (Donohoe 2010; Greenhalgh and Hurwitz 1999; Hurwitz 2000).

These truths extend further into non-Indigenous schools of thought, research, and medical education than is often apparent. For the past two decades, Michael Chandler and Chris Lalonde have published groundbreaking studies of First Nations youth suicide in British Columbia (Chandler and Lalonde 1998; Chandler et al. 2003). Their research shows that stories (otherwise called socio-cultural resiliency, competency, and continuity) are one of the single greatest preventive hedges against youth suicide in First Nations communities: if young people know their stories, if they are able to tell their own stories, they have better health outcomes. And if youth have better health outcomes, it just might be that Indigenous communities, which today experience the greatest burdens of poor health in Canada, will grow into a healthier tomorrow.

In this vein, success with ArtDays led to the design and delivery of a T-shirt printing workshop at an Indigenous Youth Conference in 2014. The workshop was designed to use arts-based methods and creative expression to re-establish positive Indigenous imagery in the hearts and minds of at-risk youth, their families, and the care providers who serve them. Using silk-screening ink, participants stencilled traditional northern and/or Aboriginal images onto plain light-grey T-shirts, along with a word infusing that image with the positive attributes the designer (and future wearer) felt it embodied in their life. The slow warm-up of teenage hearts and minds was soon

Figure 4.7   Art produced by Indigenous youth participants in a T-shirt workshop, depicting positive imagery for self-empowerment in Indigenous communities.

overwhelmed by an atmosphere of aspiration and supportive community. Participants then took these images away with them and wore the T-shirts they had created to convey these positive messages in the context of their home communities.

This T-shirt workshop was wildly successful and was offered again a short time later at an alternative high school for at-risk youth in Prince George.

Closing Reflections

Rita Charon, founder and director of the Centre for Narrative Medicine at Columbia University, articulates the basic premise of her work a little differently from King, Menard, Armstrong, Silko, Chandler, and Lalonde, whose work we have called on in this discussion: narrative stories shared between physicians (or other health care professionals) and patients, she writes, afford unique ways of navigating the most fundamental aspects of the human condition—suffering, pain, joy, fear, connection, transformation, terror, illness, death, and love, to name but a few (Charon 2006, 2004). Charon argues that narrative—the most basic scaffolding of any story, because narrative is a retelling, a description, or a relating of events in a sequential and relational way, as opposed to speaking in isolated or disjointed ways about various facets of wellness or illness—is fundamental both to meaningful clinical encounters and to human relationships (Charon 2004, 2006; see also de Leeuw 2014).

Our growing network of community partners, including Nak'azdli Health Centre, other urban, rural, and remote Indigenous agencies, and art galleries across northern BC, are full partners in arts-based research and immersion learning activities. We are therefore all invested in developing innovative, creative, and meaningful strategies that pay equal attention to the heart, mind, and body. We all want to expand practising health professionals' and medical students' understanding of Indigenous peoples, especially in northern places. As a multidisciplinary research team, we believe this increased awareness, empathy, and integration of experience and knowledge can improve recruitment and retention of health professionals in northern BC health care agencies, especially those that serve Indigenous communities and populations.

Our exploration of practices and strategies anchored in the humanities and creative arts (including painting, narration, writing, auto-ethnography, theatre, music, photography, and storytelling) is a continuous and iterative process. We are focused on transforming health care and medical education from settings *without* significant space and recognition of Indigenous conceptions of wellness and healing, cultural and spiritual aspects, or strengths and resiliencies to settings that *emphasize* holism, including psycho-social, cultural, and spiritual elements of health, cultural safety, and the privileging of Indigenous conceptions of health, well-being, and importance of place. The integration and use of Indigenous-driven creative expression with knowledges of Indigenous communities may address knowledge gaps in health decision-making and program-design processes, especially with respect to the changing landscapes of health care for Indigenous people in northern BC.

Participatory and collaborative inquiry in the spirit of ArtDays will, we hope, integrate the experiences, knowledges, and perspectives held by Indigenous peoples, community groups, and community leaders with the views of health care providers (nurses, physicians, physiotherapists, and other front-line health care workers as well as those in health promotion, social work, physiotherapy, public health, and health administration) and medical educators. Our work, at its most foundational, is evidence of the vital importance of "heart" in health and medical care, practice, research, and relationship. This work continues to grow. A gathering of HARC advisors and guiding collaborators in the Spring of 2014 at the Waap Galt'sap Longhouse at Northwest Community College Terrace Campus brought together carvers, publishers, visual artists, musicians, writers, poets, physicians, educators, actors, theatre producers, nurses and other front-line health care workers, and health researchers to consider health-arts research in the years to come. ArtDays featured prominently at this gathering, and arts-based methodologies were used to activate the hearts and minds of those gathered in envisioning a hopeful and transformative path for these "whole person" strategies—including, importantly, those of heartfelt emotionality—to engage with resiliencies and health inequities lived by Indigenous and non-Indigenous communities in northern BC. Through wholehearted consensus, this diverse group chose decolonization and decolonizing methodologies as the grounding source of direction in moving forward with this work. Emerging from this source are some of the guiding principles and veins of inquiry that will guide our practice and inquiry as we widen our northern community of practice, and as communities invite us into relationship with them. We look forward to emphasizing the primacy of cultural safety and honouring of personhood in care relationships (patient–practitioner, community–care facility, communities–health systems). We hope to build robust relationships and bodies of community-based evidence demonstrating the value of immersion education for medical students, and students in other health disciplines, in transforming primary-care relationships and improving cultural safety of care. We are working toward collaborative writing to address health inequities at multiple levels within the health care system (policy, programs, services, facilities, access, and training), and we are engaging with media at local, regional, provincial, and national levels in efforts at highlighting the need for medical humanities and the arts in medical education and health care practice. Finally, we are actively engaging with post-secondary institutions and health authorities to improve uptake of community-based evidence in transforming care, access to services, and cultural safety for Indigenous communities in northern BC and beyond. The basic model of ArtDays, anchored deeply in a commitment to heart, extends to a much broader and deeper level through the establishment of the collaborative community of practice at HARC. Arts-based methodologies are now being used, and will continue to be used, to activate the hearts of medical school deans and directors, health decision makers, local and municipal government actors, researchers outside the health disciplines, and new community-health sector partnerships in the changing landscape of health care and services provision in northern BC.

Notes

1   The term *First Nations* refers to one of three constitutionally recognized groups of Indigenous peoples in Canada—the diverse First Peoples (once called *Indians* or *Natives*) who do not identify as Métis or Inuit, Canada's two other constitutionally recognized Indigenous peoples.

2   Work in First Nations communities must adhere to particular protocols, including support from Band and Council. It's worth noting, however, that tensions exist in many communities between elected chiefs and hereditary chiefs, the former an outcome of the Indian Act of Canada and the latter a traditional structure of governance outlawed by colonial systems. Researchers and educators working with First Nations should make an effort to understand the realities of the communities with whom they are working.

CHAPTER FIVE

"Grandson, / This is meat": Hunting Metonymy in François Mandeville's *This Is What They Say*

Jasmine Spencer

1. Introduction

François Mandeville (1878–1952) was a Métis-Chipewyan trapper, fur trader, interpreter, and storyteller who lived in a region of northern Canada that is defined by Great Slave Lake to the north and Lake Athabasca to the south, connected by a system of waterways that leads, eventually, to the Arctic Sea (Bringhurst 2009, 7). Mandeville worked for the Hudson's Bay Company (HBC) until he became ill; throughout his convalescence, he built boats and trapped for himself (Scollon 2009, 228). Eventually, he returned to the HBC, retired, and passed on at the age of seventy-four in Fort Chipewyan. His was the life of a true translator; he was, in addition to a navigator of a landscape riddled with muskeg, lakes, rivers, and boreal forest, accomplished in oral and written communications and a polyglot, and thus he was also a navigator of multiple cultures and world views (229). In 1928, he narrated twenty stories to a young Chinese linguist, Li Fang-Kuei, who was seeking to study Dene languages. Five of these stories were elicited by Li (Scollon 2009, 238); they are highly pragmatic, describing how Indigenous peoples educate their youth, how to fish, how to make a canoe, how to tan a moosehide, and how to hunt beaver. But the other fifteen stories were chosen and arranged in the order of their delivery by Mandeville himself (238). Most importantly for the place where I would like to begin my analysis, Mandeville collaborated with Li on the transcriptions of those stories, editing many of the discourse markers and contributing to an exhaustive collection of paradigm slips (236–37), a textual trace of his attention to the structural qualities of the narratives. Mandeville was as fully cognisant of the way text is put to page as he was of how to live off the land and of how to negotiate cultural difference: in other words, he was aware of and adept at signification and interpretation in multiple modes—oral, written, environmental, and ontological, in the figures of animals and of their tracks and trails.[1]

Mandeville was also sensitive to literary style. He served language in both legal court contexts and liturgical church contexts (Scollon 2009, 229, 258). Indeed, Ronald Scollon, who translated Mandeville's stories from Dene Sųłiné (Chipewyan) to English twice, once in 1976 and again in 2009, writes with his research partner Suzanne Scollon that "when Li asked Mandeville for stories, Mandeville took it as an opportunity to produce his 'highest liturgical style' ... developing a 'high' or, if you prefer, literary language" (2009, 257), while Robert Bringhurst suggests, in his foreword to Scollon's 2009 translation, that

> [Mandeville's] tales of hunters and animals are Athabaskan [Dene] metaphysics incarnate. He achieved, with the Chipewyan language, the kind of symbiotic relationship that literature demands. He knew not just the meanings of the words, the permutations of the verb, and the syntax of the sentence. He had learned the motivic form of those much larger units of Chipewyan thought that we call stories. This made it possible for Mandeville and the stories to speak through one another, and that is what they did. (Bringhurst 2009, 10)

"Metaphysics incarnate": this phrase leads me to consider the incarnate, the carnal, further. The carnal, the fleshly, sensuous, embodied, material: what does this mean in narratives that are, after all, patterns of thought that inhere—are incarnated—in the mind or on the page, neither of which is "motivic" in the usual musical or mechanical senses? In a literary sense, Mandeville's narratives have been, and continue to be, intensely mobile; or, if the stories are not mobile, they motivate the minds and bodies of their hearers and readers to carry them around. Historically, Mandeville's narratives have circulated the sub-Arctic, made their way to the eastern seaboard of the United States, to Hawaii, to Taipei, and, now, again, to Canada (Mandeville 1976, 2009). And that is just in terms of their printed circulation; oral versions of these narratives were told before Mandeville's time and still are very much in use in northern Dene communities.[2] So Mandeville's conversation with these narratives infiltrates and reverberates within the imaginations of those who encounter them.[3] The conversation continues, but the entities participant in it have yet to be well defined.

I am particularly interested in the idea of the "carnal" in Mandeville's narratives because flesh, particularly animal flesh[4]—meat and the eating of meat—is such an important motif in almost all the narratives. For the corollary to the presence of flesh is ingestion, and this is a pattern that recurs throughout Mandeville's narratives: flesh and ingestion. In the north, hunting, trapping, snaring, and fishing were—and, many argue, remain—essential to survival. But if Bringhurst is correct in asserting that Mandeville's narratives are Dene metaphysics incarnate (and their intensely communicable qualities suggest to me that this must be so), then "meat," while the essence of bodily survival, must imply much more than metabolic fuel; meat or flesh animates the narratives at the level of structure, such that the plots themselves "ingest"—and sometimes regurgitate—the stuff of their own making.

Perhaps Bringhurst has read Maurice Merleau-Ponty on the phenomenology of flesh:

> flesh is not matter, is not mind, is not substance. To designate it, we should need the old term "element," in the sense it was used to speak of water, air, earth, and fire, that is, in the sense of a *general thing*, midway between the spatio-temporal individual and the idea, a sort of incarnate principle that brings a style of being wherever there is a fragment of being. (Merleau-Ponty [ca. 1960] 1968, 256)

Flesh is a "style of being wherever there is a fragment of being": this is an assertion I would like to take seriously with respect to Mandeville's stories, because it evokes a kind of metaphysical frame metonymy, a figure structuring thought where source and target are both materially and conceptually incarnate and mutually interpenetrating. And if I have learned anything from Mandeville's narratives, it is that ethics and aesthetics both are interpenetrating, inherent in the metaphysics and the pragmatics of narrative, and essential to survival.[5]

Metonymical structure requires a sense of the whole as well as of the interconnection of its parts, a sense of transformation that retains its origins even as it moves. In Mandeville's narrative "The Man Who Became a Wolf," for example, ontological survival is premised on embodied and interpenetrating relationships between wolf and humanity. Such relationships or connections lead to the renewal of the protagonist's life through his transformation into a wolf—and back again—and through the discursive and embodied transformation of tracks into meat: of hoofprints in the bush into caribou or moose, and of caribou or moose into meat or food. In other words, the *this* in "Grandson, / this is meat" refers not to the animal but to its trace, a discursive trace that enacts its embodiment as food. Just as Mandeville's work with Li crosses disciplinary, linguistic, and cultural boundaries, this narrative enacts its own meaning, revealing metonymical connections in the mind and in the material world in the mouth. This is because the word for *caribou*, in Dene Sųłiné, is *ʔetθén*,[6] which is the same as the word for *meat* or *flesh*.[7] These words come from the same places in the tongue and teeth. They are breathed into and spat out of the mouth in the same order. They talk to each other in that cave. By encompassing one another, so that prey is always already food through the work of interpretation, the signs—the words for animal tracks and the animal tracks—become sustenance—meat. This is one of Mandeville's messages in this story, a message that becomes very good "eatin'" in, I think, both source and target languages—in translation.[8] As Jacques Rancière (1987, 11) writes, this is translation "under the sign of equality," whereby interpretation—and the teaching of the skills necessary to interpretation—reveals that "all sentences, and consequently all intelligences that produce them, are of the same nature," so that "understanding is never more than translating, that is, giving the equivalent of a text, but in no way its reason" (9). "In no way its reason": the reason that *ʔetθén* works with itself in the story is not merely aesthetic; but also practical. But how does this shared lexical quality permit practical as well as conceptual exchange beyond the body of the animal, through its tracks on the land, into its *narrative* traces—through inter-semiotic transformations? Whereas Roman Jacobson (1966, 233) defines inter-semiotic translation as an "interpretation of verbal signs by means of signs of non-verbal sign systems" (233), Mandeville begins with the interpretation of non-verbal signs by means of verbal signs. If there is "no *signatum* [meaning] without *signum* [sign]" (Jacobson 1966, 232), then Mandeville's homophony becomes sustenance. But how do words come alive—or reveal themselves to be already alive—in Mandeville's stories? How does he make visible the interconnections between words and wisdom? How does he embody—make flesh—his intelligence? In the following section, I use the concept of *frame metonymy* from cognitive linguistic theory to explore the connections between the oral and the embodied, the track and the animal.

2. Frame Metonymy

I use the cognitive linguistic theory of frame metonymy to analyze the meat of Mandeville's narratives because this theoretical approach is flexible yet highly specific, much as a hunter's approach to navigating the muskeg must be. My analysis is meant to be an individual response to this story, which inspires as many responses as there are listeners to and readers of it. At the same time, there are at least two well-defined examples at a grammatical level in which animals, or their tracks and trails, metonymically refer to meat: "His meat is certainly here" references a living bear in his den (Mandeville 2009, 130),[9] while, as I describe above, a wolf says, "Grandson, / this is meat" in reference to some moose tracks (162). These sentence-level examples are visible evidence of some of the interconnected parts of Mandeville's larger narrative principles that I engage with below. The abilities of the storytellers engaged with in this collection to deploy complex verbal patterns is something that must be accepted as creative, insightful, and strategic, as Patrick Moore discusses in his chapter on the value of code-switching (see chapter 1, this volume) and as Bren Kolson describes so beautifully in chapter 8, on the storyteller Old Rawhide.

Klaus-Uwe Panther (2006, 147) provides a definition of frame metonymy that draws on cognitive linguistic research and semiotics: "metonymy is an indexical relation between source and target meaning." He fleshes out this indexicality by suggesting that "metonymy is a kind of meaning elaboration whose result is a conceptually prominent target meaning, an integrated whole that contains the backgrounded source meaning and novel meaning components resulting from the process of elaboration" (147), such that the "target meaning resulting from a metonymic shift is an elaboration of the source meaning" (151). This "metonymic shift can be regarded as a substitution operation, but one in which the source meaning does not vanish but remains part of the conceptual structure of the target meaning" (151). These points are salient not only for the emphasis they place on discursive metonymy as a retroductive cognitive phenomenon but also because narratives, in Mandeville's milieu, provide important information for physical as well as social survival:

it is unwise, in the immediacy of survival in the north, to identify some components of narrative discourse as real and dismiss the rest as unreal.[10]

To fully define my usage of animal referentiality within frame metonymy, I shall adopt two additional points from Panther's discussion of metonymy. First, metonymical source and target are often structures that elaborate segments of concepts, not always entire domains:

> In elaborating a source concept, metonymy relies in general on pre-established inferential patterns. The kinds of conceptual realms in which metonymic shifts operate are not necessarily whole cognitive domains (and subdomains) stored in long-term memory, but they might be more like mental spaces, i.e., "small conceptual packets constructed as we think and talk, for purposes of local understanding and action" (Fauconnier and Turner 2002: 40). (Panther 2006, 161)

Here Panther makes the point that elaboration is a matter of referencing and networking mental spaces, or "conceptual packets," a cognitive phenomenon not unlike Bringhurst's narrative motifs but with the additional parameter of anatomy, as it were: sometimes the flesh of the narrative operates by parts, not wholes—by intermittent analogies, not just zoological realities—by moving to change one's position for the revivification of muscle with breath. Panther also makes the point that elaboration by way of these domains and subdomains, or "packets" of "local" relations, is often "a matter of perspective," in that the scholar may or may not be immediately or wholly able to determine "what to regard as the superordinate domain and what as the subdomain(s), respectively" (Panther 2006, 158). I find this point particularly salient in relation to Mandeville's animal referentiality because position—geographical, ontological—as a determiner of meaning seems to be very fluid in the narratives. What I mean by this kind of *position* has to do with relations or even alliances between species—human and caribou, human and wolf—but also between much more conceptual values, such as ingestion and projection (who or what is eating whom or what?) or, even more abstractly, predation and perpetuation (which comes first, destruction or renewal?). These values seem to come into dual focus thanks to frames defined by the contiguities (spatial relations) and contingencies (temporal relations) of lived experience—where entities are brought together by environmental factors such as landscape or the cycles of seasons, but also by more fragmented yet syllogistic visual analogues, such as colour and texture, or even in moments of fury or of song, or in acts such as the donning of human clothing, or in hibernation.

Thus existential (contiguous and contingent) as well as ontological (morphological) states seem to be a major factor in overlapping frames and generating blends. So which predicates which: narrative contiguity and contingency or narrative analogy? The key to understanding the structure and directionality of Mandeville's unique metonymies is found in examining the total context of their deployment—their total ecological topography. Barbara Dancygier's definition of frame metonymy expands upon Panther's point about metonymical "elaboration" by showing that narratives provide powerful contexts for indexing between source and target. Frame metonymy, she writes, is a "set of directional associations between culturally-rich concepts, or domains, that are activated by combining lexical and grammatical entities through narrative" (Dancygier 2011, 33). Further, she states that frame metonymy as a narrative schema can help to generate the emerging meaning of a story, because frame metonymy is a

> situation whereby a reference is made to an aspect of a culturally salient frame, but the listener/reader is prompted to think of a network of culturally valid concepts and use it in processing ... the dual foci of the frame are connected in experience ... The nature of ... transformation ... is the crux of (I think) a broader frame ... overlapping metonymically evoked frames lead to new blends. (Barbara Dancygier, personal communication, 31 March 2013)

This definition has four key components that specifically address the structure of frame metonymy in a cross-cultural context: (1) reference, (2) cultural frame, (3) networks, and (4) transformative blends. In Figure 5.1, I propose to apply this metonymical template, with its core idea of the frame as a transformative dual foci, to Mandeville's metonymical narrative structures.

There is one additional component—an "incarnate principle"—that underlies, "midway between the spatio-temporal individual and the idea," all four components: (5) some latent ground or conceptualization of lived experience. This latent ground is laid, I believe, by Mandeville's narrative topography—the verbal signs of his narrative collection or "cycle," as it has

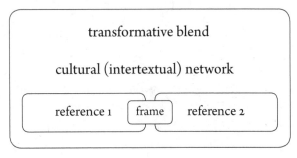

FIGURE 5.1

been titled, that construe the "nonverbal sign systems" of lived experience by permitting the listener or reader to experience his story world as its own ground for inter-semiotic as intertextual transformation.

Panther (2006, 148) writes of lived experience that "metonymic meanings provide generic prompts that are fleshed out on the basis of background knowledge (world knowledge), the situation of the utterance and the linguistic context (co-text) in which the metonymic expression occurs." As a southern student of literature, I do not find it easy to define all that lived experience entails for Dene inhabitants of the north, especially as it would have been during a time of great transition such as that which Mandeville witnessed. However, Mandeville's story collection—or "story cycle," as the subtitle of Scollon's 2009 translation suggests—offers a rich array of literary—"inter-semiotic"—life experience as a context for interpretation. After all, Mandeville states in the first of his elicited narratives, "Education," that

> It's been said that our people didn't teach each other,
> but that isn't true.
> We have always taught each other.
> Now I will tell you how people taught each other. (Mandeville 2009, 199)

He then proceeds to orate and transcribe narratives that overwhelmingly concern meat and the source of meat: animals.

In order to work towards a view of the narrative "situation of the utterance and the linguistic context ('co-text') in which the metonymic expression occurs" (Panther 2006, 148), then, I shall next summarize my findings of the work of the two large game animals, caribou and moose, and then conclude by applying the schema of frame metonymy to "meat" as it is embodied by these animals, which are the most "meaty" of sources of sustenance for hunters in the north. I shall focus my "experience" of the presence of and narrative frames evoked by caribou and moose,[11] who compose "meat" in the pragmatic sense, because they also operate in especially transformative ways, in story 1, "How Copper Was Discovered" (Mandeville 2009, 19–31) and story 11, "The Man Who Became a Wolf" (157–73). These animals serve as such—animals, biologically bound creatures whose personal lives intersect in realistic landscapes with those of the protagonists—but also as "fragments of being" that evoke the dual foci of intertextual comparison in which the components of frame metonymy—(1) reference, (2) cultural frame, (3) networks, and (4) transformative blends—inform one another mutually, that is, in an intertextually lively manner.[12] In analyzing the presence of caribou and moose in Mandeville's cycle, I hope to trace an emergent set of textually salient cultural frames for these animals—and thus to come to understand better their motivic blending through metonymical referencing; in this way, I hope eventually to touch upon and to touch narrative animals as carnal matrices of Mandeville's story cycle, where life and death—predation and perpetuation, affinity and affiliation—are worked out in mythopoeic ways. The motif that ultimately emerges, I anticipate, will be that of "flesh" in Merleau-Ponty's sense, but inflected peculiarly by Mandeville as "meat" to evoke and work through the hermeneutics of ecological transformation—of contiguity and contingency—as an interpretive problem within lived experience.

3. Meat

Caribou appear in nine of the stories in Mandeville's story cycle (1–4, 6–8, 10, and 11). Of these appearances, some of the most significant occur in the first story, "How Copper Was Discovered" (Mandeville 2009, 19–31); in this story, caribou serve as guides to Copper Woman, a woman captured by enemies who runs away from them through an unfamiliar landscape. At the beginning of her flight, at the shore of the ocean, Copper Woman carefully observes caribou migrating through the water and decides that because the caribou are almost always walking, not swimming, she can follow them (12–25). Later, one caribou from the herd she follows serves as a source of meat for her; she spears, butchers, and cures the meat by laying it out on the ground to dry (25–27). Later still, when she notices a bright light in the sky and walks towards it (abandoning both the route of the migrating caribou and her son by her enemy), she discovers "native copper" (naturally occurring chunks of copper) lying on the ground that resembles meat (26, 28–29). After this point, her journey turns from the horizon and goes downwards when she is raped by some men whom she guides to the copper despite having enjoined them to act in a good way (30). Because she is angry, she and the copper sink down into the earth in four increments—the copper and Copper Woman become less and less visible and available until they are completely gone, hidden underground and therefore unattainable (30–31).

In story 2, "How Iron Was Discovered" (32–36), caribou trails guide Beaver Orphan, a powerful man, and his people to meat on the shore of the northern ocean, in the barren land, in the same territory of the enemies who took Copper Woman (32). Beaver Orphan and his people discover caribou for meat (33) and then chunks of iron, a material that initially, for them, bears only a partial analogy to more familiar materials such as stone and wood (33). The discovery of iron goes differently than that of copper: Beaver Orphan has a dream that guides him to sing over the iron, blow on it, and so split the hunk into more workable pieces (34–35). From these "small pieces like wood" (35), the people make arrowheads and spear-points (35–36). So the metonymical process at work in story 1 can be schematized as follows: (1) trail; (2) guide, meat; (3) new alliance (with metal); (4) new environment. In story 2, the process is (1) trail, (2) meat, (3) new encounter (with metal), (4) new weaponry (arrowheads and spear-points for hunting and warring).

In stories 3 and 4, "Raven Head" (37–71) and "His Grandmother Raised Him" (72–74), tribal fortunes likewise change because of the absence or presence of caribou, but rather than caribou bodies serving as guides to migration, or their trails serving as guides to meat towards innovations in technology, caribou in these two stories serve to form new kinds of human community. "Raven Head," told in four parts (an important number in Dene cognition), vividly depicts conflicts between leader and followers, brother and sister, and one tribe with another. The protagonist, Raven Head, is something of a trickster figure[13] who rises in power in the first two parts of the story and falls and dies in the latter two; caribou appear at the end of the second part of the story. Raven Head tells his brother that their dead relatives spear caribou "up north / at a caribou crossing" on the sandy edge of a lake (60), so the trickster and his brother canoe to "lake with the caribou crossing" to be with their dead relatives, including their mother and father (60). Part two of the story ends with a short epilogue: "If people have done no wrong, when they die / they go to that place where Raven Head / and his brother canoed. This is what they say" (61).

Story 4, "His Grandmother Raised Him," was narrated by Baptiste Forcier, an elder in Mandeville's community in Fort Chipewyan; Mandeville, believing Forcier to be a superior storyteller, chose the story and asked Forcier to narrate it to Li (Scollon 2009, 237). In this story, the protagonist, His Grandmother Raised Him, takes his grandmother away from a group of people who displeased him (72) and then goes and lives with caribou for a long time (73). When he returns to her, he brings a belt full of caribou tongues for them to eat (73). In another version of the story, told by Fred Marcel (who is from the same community as Mandeville), the protagonist "was found in the moss by his grandmother" and that he "killed caribou by biting the end of their tongues" (Scollon 2009, 259–60). The presence and power of the tongue is intriguing: it suggests that the extraction of parts from metonymical wholes is transformative. Compare the extraction of body parts from wholes with the suction of blood from the body in order to become a better hunter in a Dene culture adjacent to Dene Sųłiné, the Dane-zaa (Beaver), whose territory lies on the border between Alberta and British Columbia. A spiritual guide—"a big fat man" (Ridington and Ridington 2006, 155)—teaches a hunter to go under the earth and form an affinity with his prey by sucking on the hunter's forehead until he draws blood.[14] In the mythic system of the Dane-zaa, all animals originate from giant animals who live under the earth (Ridington 1978, 65). Robin Ridington comments that a "moose lick is a place where, the Dane-zaa say, the bodies of moose emerge from beneath the earth. It is a cosmic center where game trails converge and change direction. It is a place of shamanic transformation," and, just as the "initiate [the hunter led by the big fat man] himself passes through the portal of the moose lick, a place where moose lips touch the earth," so the shamanic "lick sucks an initiate inside itself and into another world" (Ridington and Ridington 2006, 236). The acts of sucking blood and eating, perhaps even biting out, caribou tongues in these stories are, I think, analogous ritual acts upon transformative bodily thresholds that induce fleshly affinity with animals. This latter story in particular illustrates the power of the mouth as a source of life—in a sense, words are small animals that emerge from the cavern of the larger. But sucking is an act of atomic transfusion across membranes or transfiguration across boundaries. Biting, on the other hand, is a muscular cross-boundary act of ingestion leading not merely to exchange by passing through a portal from human to animal but, rather, to an aggressive internalization of the liminal threshold itself to induce total transformation, where that which once resided on the distal side of the boundary is drawn through to the aggressor's proximal side of the boundary. In Forcier's story, His Grandmother Raised Him and his grandmother return to the caribou, who, tongueless, have died by a lake; the old woman butchers and dries all the meat, which they then take to the protagonist's uncle's community to make a new life—and "since that time the caribou have lived together with people" (Mandeville 2009, 74). So in story 3, the schema for caribou is (1) lakeside crossing, (2) meat, (3) new camp, (4) new life (heavenly); in story 4 it is (1) tongues ingested, (2) meat, (3) new species alliance, (4) new human community with a new way of life.

In stories 6 and 7, "Old Axe—Story One" (93–105) and "Old Axe—Story Two" (106–16), the protagonist, Old Axe, suggests that his people invade another people's territory because there are lots of caribou and fish in that territory (story 6, 101), thanks to the presence of a caribou crossing on a large lake full of fish (story 7, 106). Both stories involve the prospect of aggressive migration into others' territories for access to caribou migration. In story 8, "The Cannibal" (117–24), a human is captured by the Cannibal in an invisible snare and pretends to be dead when the Cannibal finds him (117). The Cannibal ties him up in "sunbeams" (117) and carries his prey home, where his children call the human man "his [the Cannibal's] caribou" and warn their father that he is "coming back to life" and escaping (119). This story suggests two things: one, that "animality" does not always predicate "meat": rather, animality is sometimes a subcategory or subdomain of meat—to be prey is to be animal—to be signum is to be signatum. What a "caribou" is in a figurative sense, then, depends on who is hunting and who is being hunted. So in story 6, caribou work as (1) trails, (2) meat, (3) invasion and takeover, (4) new territory; in story 7, caribou work following the same sequence. And in story 8, caribou work as (1) prey, (2) meat, (3) mutual predation, (4) undesirable new species that infiltrates the territories of skin itself.

Story 10, like stories 6 and 7, involves caribou trails and conflict; in "The Adventures of Beaulieu" (133–56), the protagonists, Mandeville and Beaulieu, infiltrate a camp of people by saying that they got lost hunting caribou because they could not find any tracks where they came from (140). These three stories suggest that caribou tracks and trails cross human camp and territorial boundaries in politically destabilizing ways. This destabilizing phenomenon also suggests that camps and lakeshores intersect with trails in a schematic sense: they are, as Panther suggests, "mental spaces" that "tap portions of frames stored in long-term memory," so that "whenever a metonymic operation takes place a whole conceptual frame is activated" (Panther 2006, 161). This activation occurs when camp boundaries are penetrated by caribou tracks or trails and by those following them. Beaulieu and Mandeville also hunt moose, a high-stakes, high-yield game meat that increases their social leverage in the camp because they become a supply of meat even as they consume others' supplies of meat (Mandeville 2009, 144, 152–54). Thus, caribou/moose function in story 10 as (1) trails, (2) meat, (3) invasion and takeover, (4) new community.

In the final story featuring caribou in Mandeville's cycle, story 11, "The Man Who Became a Wolf" (157–73), caribou—and also moose—serve as prey for wolves. The ontological status of the wolves is defined by their relation to one another as hunters; the protagonist, Spread Wings, is actually a human man who has the special ability to transform into a wolf when he is old and in need of renewal—he "from time to time became a wolf. This is what they say" (157). When he becomes old on one occasion, a wolf who is always a wolf approaches him and speaks to him to remind him that "If you want to live longer on the earth / you must live with us again" (157). Spread Wings is initially reluctant—he "thought, 'I don't want to be a wolf again'"—and although he only thought the words, the wolf answers him by stating that if he does not, he will die soon (157). Spread Wings realizes that he "want[s] to live longer on this earth" (157), and so "He immediately became a wolf" (158). This crisscrossing between discursive speech–thought–speech and human–wolf–human communication leads to utterance so powerful it becomes relational ontology: Spread Wings says "I will become a wolf again" (157), and instantly he does so—a chiasm between desire and transformation comparable to the relationship between fury and sinking down for Copper Woman, or between biting and eating caribou tongues for His Grandmother Raised Him.

It is only once Spread Wings has assented to becoming, and so becomes, a wolf that he realizes the wolf who is always a wolf is actually an old woman. She addresses him as "grandson" and guides him north to hunt caribou (158).

Spread Wings's reluctance to transform into a wolf becomes understandable in the narrative that follows: it is always difficult for them to find meat. But not only does the grandmother/wolf guide Spread Wings to meat, she also teaches him how to hunt caribou, to eat it slowly so as not to become ill, to howl or sing for others who may be nearby and hungry to share in the game, and to cache the excess meat in the snow for others to use if they are hungry (158–61). This suggests to me that although Spread Wings has become a wolf before, he must relearn each time he transforms how to hunt and survive. Such skills are a matter of pragmatic survival, to be sure, but they are also, more conceptually, a kind of epistemological movement across ontological boundaries where that which is known is peculiar to, and therefore predicated by, species-specific relations (i.e., to "herds" or "packs"—or to human "camps"). Movement for transformative knowing demands—must be predicated by—trans-species affinity: so a wolf becomes a grandmother, or, perhaps more accurately, a human becomes a wolf's pup.

Moose occur less frequently than caribou in Mandeville's story cycle, but they are an integral part of Spread Wings's story. After hunting caribou for some time, he and the grandmother/wolf come to find it extremely difficult to find meat. They begin to starve. At last, the grandmother/wolf guides Spread Wings away from the barren land and into the forest to look for moose (162). Moose are more difficult to find because they make tracks, not trails (less permanent signs according to less predictable foraging movements), and are also much, much larger and therefore more difficult to kill, even using the cooperative hunting techniques that the grandmother/wolf teaches Spread Wings. In the woods, however, the grandmother/wolf eventually finds moose tracks, and says, "Grandson, / this is meat" (162). The triumph and assurance implied by this metonymical statement is predicated upon hunters in difficult hermeneutical situations in all the stories leading up to this one; just as Copper Woman, Raven Head and his younger brother, His Grandmother Raised Him and his grandmother, Old Axe, and the two Métis looking for a camp to make their own persist in seeking sustenance by observing and then manipulating the natural and social metaphysics of their environments,[15] so do the wolves. The moose they catch together by its leg tendon, nose, and belly (163–64) is meat intensified. It is harder to catch and kill, and it must be consumed in even more explicitly incremental substances than caribou—first, the wolves are to drink the blood; second, to eat some muscle; third, and only after their stomachs have readjusted to food, to eat some fat; and fourth, they must howl or sing for others who may be hungry to join them (164–65). This high-stakes meat demands an anatomy of ingestion that is three parts flesh and one part social.

In the latter portion of "The Man Who Became a Wolf," the grandmother/ wolf reproduces (but not with Spread Wings), and together they teach her pups to hunt caribou in the winter (169) and moose in the spring or summer (169–71). They hunt and sing until meat again becomes scarce. This time, the grandmother/wolf sends Spread Wings back to his own "pack," which is to say the camp of his own species. Her pack is weak from hunger and could use his hunting skills, yet the grandmother/wolf—who is also, now, a mother by filiation as well as a grandmother by affinity—tells Spread Wings to go back to live with his relatives and to always leave a little meat for wolves when he hunts and kills: "remember this as long as you live when you kill something" (172). She then says, "Now we'll sing, / and then you go back to your people" (172). And so "They all sang for him, / and then Spread Wings left them" (172). Just as Mandeville's wordplay fills the mouth with food (ʔɛtθén) so that homophony becomes sustenance, the wolves' polyphonic song is shown to fill the muskeg with the inter-semiotic—yet metonymically unified—transformations necessary not just for their own survival but also for others' survival.

Spread Wings's transition back to humanity, then, seems to follow from two events: first, a deliberately self-aware yet selfless animal sacrifice; and, second, human retention of the principle of sacrifice learned while allied with the animal, for Spread Wings and his kin are always to remember to leave a sampling—a signature—of meat for his affiliative kind. So Spread Wings retains a "style of being" by reserving a "fragment of being" (meat) for wolves as he becomes emergent from wolves, although he could not do the opposite (retain hunting techniques in his shift from human to wolf in the first place). This suggests to me that humanity depends on animality for survival as ethics but also for direction in the aesthetics of living—that is, empathy through sacrifice but also communal discourse raised to the affective excess of song, an excess of homophony and polyphony that takes the human back to itself by way of the animal.

Spread Wings, who encounters a lone human on the edge of a lake, approaches "on four legs" (172) and speaks to the human, explaining that he is one of his own. Although the man is scared and has a gun, he does not shoot (173); instead, he quietly goes back to his home and brings Spread Wings human clothing, saying nothing to his human co-inhabitants (173). Spread Wings goes into the woods to don this clothing and emerges human; together, they go "back to the people," and Spread Wings tells them "about how he had been a wolf"—and "that's how he became a person again" (173). Thus caribou/moose in story 11 might be said to follow the schema (1) trails and tracks, (2) meat, (3) new species alliance, (4) new hunting practices and new body.

4. Discussion and Conclusion

To summarize cumulatively, then, using the four key components of frame metonymy—(1) reference, (2) cultural frame, (3) networks, (4) transformative blends—caribou/moose across Mandeville's narratives can be observed most often to move from a reference by (1) signs, symbolic trails, or tracks to (2) signify the cultural frame of *meat*, or sustenance, whether animate and on the move or butchered, eaten, shared, and cached; this leads to (3) networks of transformation between groups—herds, camps, swarms, packs—whenever a protagonist comes into contact with a caribou or moose, in order to (4) bring two points of view together and achieve transformation. Ultimately, I think this transformation leads to the generic space (5) phenomenological flesh as a mutable perpetuation of multiple ways of being that are predational according to relational rules of sacrifice—in the sense of becoming animal, and of becoming human.

The target frame *meat* evoked by the source *trails* brings disparate species into dual focus to generate networks of predation and perpetuation that might be characterized by *alliance* (affinity, affiliation, extension, elaboration, transfusion, transfiguration, transformation). These networks operate within and between the narratives by coeval contradistinctions, that is, by overlapping frames to produce co-texts—"co(n)texts," in other words. For example, tribes are defined by different languages spoken (story 1), caribou meat and native copper by the surfaces and depths of the earth (story 1), iron from wood (story 2), the before life from the after life (story 3), human comestibles from non-human comestibles (stories 4 and 8), the leader's loyalty towards his chosen camp versus false affiliation with his target (enemy) camp (stories 6 and 7), warm-blooded beings from parasitic swarms (story 8), allied individuals and divided camps (story 10), and wolf packs from human settlements (story 11). The one constant, *meat*—the cultural frame (2) always evoked by variable references (1)—thus emerges as a consistent metonymic target domain emerging from networks (3) coordinated by opposing yet overlapping nexuses that come into dual focus, often through bodily exchanges (in whole or part) to generate transformative blends (4)— blends that are the product of intensive, almost volcanic, fusions and fissions between ontological positions.

These fusions and fissions operate through environmental contingencies, conducted by caribou trails and moose tracks and by cognitive analogies between like and unlike—culture and language, colours and shapes, textures, life and death, physical anatomy, spraying blood and swarming insects, charisma, and the ethics and aesthetics of hunting. But to return to a question I ask above—which predicates which, contingency and contiguity or analogy?—I would like to suggest that the mutual semiological interdependence that always characterizes the emergent ground of meaning in Mandeville's transformative narrative syntax ultimately demands mental agility—analogical thinking—before, but not exclusive of, experiential ability—mastery of ecological contiguity and contingency. Panther suggests that

> metonymy involves semantic contiguity, which manifests itself as positional similarity ... The metonymic operation occurs in a specific syntactic position in the sentence and is therefore paradigmatic, but the relation between the metonymic source and its target is one of semantic contiguity. (2006, 150)

He elaborates by proposing that "if it is assumed that metonymy is a case of indexicality, the contingence of the metonymic relation follows automatically" (155). In the context of Mandeville's story cycle, however, it seems to me that both contiguity and contingency between competing species in a challenging physical environment compete with multivalent analogy in an equally challenging discursive mental environment. Thus there are no automatic allies, only alliances formed by great struggle between analogical entities that converge and diverge to generate their interdependent significations. For Mandeville, then, just as meat and story are interdependently constructed, interdependent hermeneutics require deeply analogical creative construals of contingency and contiguity. These construals are mental "packets" that mutually index each other.

While the scope of this chapter permits only a sampling of the work of animals in Mandeville's narratives, I suggest some domains or mental packets conjoined by networks such as caribou trails and moose tracks in the stories: planes—sea, ice, barren land/muskeg, forest, perhaps sky; circles—tribe, herd, metal mine, stomach, shoreline, inlet, lake, snare, net, camp, tent, firepit, skull/brain, swarm, pack, den, cache; and centres that are penetrated—a woman's body by rape, lakes by canoes, mouths by tongues removed, atomized skulls by fire and club, forest groves by tracks, packs by song. So, to return to the metonymical structure predicated on the core idea of dual focus, Merleau-Ponty's proposition that flesh as a "style of being wherever there is a fragment of being" ([ca. 1960] 1968, 256) is, in Mandeville's story cycle, growth that blends perspective or position between domains or packets with attributes that are defined by exchange—a sort of inter-semiotic transfusion—between interior and exterior, not just between biological species or chemical compositions or even instrumental functions.

In Figure 5.2, the ground from which the transformative blend of meaning that emerges from meat as flesh may be described not only as interior/exterior but as emergent from networks between containment and penetration, ingestion and regurgitation, extension and intension, or predation and perpetuation. I call this *ground flesh*, flesh brought into revealing by the hunter (interpreter), because flesh signifies the "connective tissue of exterior and interior horizons" (Merleau-Ponty [ca. 1960] 1968, 131) that storytelling demands. Because hunting is a transitional or peripheral activity, like sickness, rape, and death, it enacts and thus makes visible the connective tissue that narrative brings forth. In other words, hunters go beyond the edge of their camp or herd or swarm or pack, where they encounter the edge of another "herd"; the boundaries between groups blur in the process, which is hard work requiring predictive empathy for the quarry so radical that often the hunter merges with and emerges from her or his prey. Figuratively, Mandeville hunts the inner animal across the convex horizon of the skull; in hunting it, he becomes it, inverting the inner horizon to become an ever-concaving extension of his lived physical and conceptual environment.

Mandeville's story cycle, then—its cursive artistry, its verbal specificities, and its intertextual sequencing—is a working translation, a translation that works for its transformation, a kind of hunting that moves between the fissions and fusions of spoken and written language. It is an intertextual text,

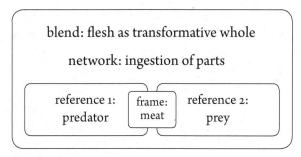

blend: flesh as transformative whole

network: ingestion of parts

reference 1: predator

frame: meat

reference 2: prey

FIGURE 5.2

a body of narrative in which predator and prey encompass one another "to speak through one another," as Bringhurst (2009, 10) puts it, demonstrating how verbal and non-verbal signs encompass, engulf, ingest one another—for there is no signatum without the signum, but there is also no sign without its meaning. One animal needs another. Thus Mandeville's story cycle has the potential to make a zoology of humanity; this is his "motivic" ontology, the movement of cognitive positions and of movement between positions. If so, Mandeville's theory of humanity and animality—constructed by and between perspectives cursive, discursive, incursive, recursive—"meat" that is flesh self-aware, not merely a "thing, but a possibility, a latency" that, recurved in narrative form, becomes a "veritable touching of the touch" (Merleau-Ponty [ca. 1960] 1968, 133)—is as complex as and comparable to the insights of other philosophers of being. Michel Foucault's "zoophyte"— where "place and similitude become entangled" and "we see mosses growing on the outsides of shells, plants in the antlers of stags, a sort of grass on the faces of men" to make some manner of "strange zoophyte" that, "by mingling together the properties that make it similar to the plants as well as to the animals, also juxtaposes them" (Foucault [1966] 1970, 20–21); Jacques Derrida's "l'animot"—the animal-word that seeks to "open … onto the referential experience of the thing as such, as what it is in its being" ([1997] 2002, 416); and even Gilles Deleuze and Félix Guattari's "anomal" (1980, 42), which is constituted by an "alliance or the pact" that is a "form of expression for an infection or epidemic constituting the form of content" (45) in order to "border each multiplicity," to be the "precondition for the alliance necessary to becoming," and to carr[y] the transformation of becoming or crossings of multiplicities always farther down the line of flight" (46–47)—all advocate a similar textual ecology, although none of their works could guide a hungry hunter to meat in the tundra. So Mandeville's narratives constitute a uniquely northern mode of becoming animal—that is to say, becoming new through ever-new relations. His metonymical alliances lead to new forms, to a metonymical form of forms that is forever in conversation with itself, forever translating breath and words and blood and flesh between enemies and allies.

In traditional Dene hunting practices, a man who wants to hunt successfully sleeps with his head towards the rising sun, so that the approaching light will cast his dream self forward onto the right trails to find meat (Ridington 1990, 69). And Dene hunters can find in their dreams the "source of trails and the origin of game" (Brody [1981] 2004, 45). Good hunting depends on knowing these trails (45). Those who have the skill of dream-hunting can also tell others how to find trails to "get to heaven" while avoiding "wrong trails"— "heaven is to one side of, and at the same level as, the point where the trails to animals all meet" (47). Perhaps similarly, then, Mandeville is a hunter who stands in front of a sun that is story; his narrative shadow streams in front of him as the hermeneutic incarnate, as game that goes before him on a trail that travels between and across all the world's boundaries—like and unlike Dante's Virgil. Likewise, Copper Woman stands on the shore and looks out across the horizon to observe that "caribou are walking across the ocean, / but they don't come back" (Mandeville 2009, 23). As she contemplates leaving her captors, she reasons that although "there is no land [she] can see in that direction," there "must be land lying right underneath the surface" (23). Thus she decides, "I'll follow the caribou," for "If I die, I am not with my relatives anyway" (23). And when a wolf follows game spoor to say, "Grandson, / this is meat," the utterance signifies that moments of death or near death are recurrent nexuses of exchange. This is why a hunter endures bloodletting by a "big fat man"—so that he can "renew contact with the animals and continue the hunter's 'holy occupation' of transforming animals into human food" (Ridington and Ridington 2006, 244). There is, in Dene poetics, a bloody relationship between enemies and allies—the line between enemy and ally seems to follow not categories of kin, filiation, or language but, rather, broad, cyclical movements between fleshly and meaty domains. This continual form of return is essential to Mandeville's symbiotic metaphysics of life and death. There is forever a sinking down and a rising up, a going in and a coming out. These stories are reincarnation embodied, as an ever-unfinished migration between contiguity and contingency and analogy, necessity and dream, a hermeneutics of sacrifice for working through the interpretive problem that is lived experience.

If this is so, then the human as a positional construal of narrative topography must constantly be rearticulated; it is constantly shifting with letters on the page and oral sequences and migrating caribou that follow patterns according to a germ of articulation—syllogism, schema, anatomy—so that that which is inner, flesh, is exposed as meat, sustenance, and that which is exposed becomes hidden. The word *Ɂɛtθén* is one example of how language draws to the attention of the listener or reader of Mandeville's narratives the unity and translatability of the world within itself, for itself, by itself. In a way, teaching listeners and readers how to read is one of Mandeville's many objectives. But it is not just reading. He teaches his listeners and readers how to translate. Mandeville advocates a hermeneutics of inter-semiotic translation—in Jacobson's words, this is a form of "inter-semiotic" translation that is really *"transmutation"* (1966, 233), a transmutation fully embodied, translation made flesh, wherein hunger for the word and hunger in the world motivate cognitive exchanges between species—human and wolf—as signs that indicate a shifting of radically different perspectives. Perhaps the point is not so much where one ends up but that one is in motion—a point of view very much in keeping with the work of literary interpretation and with lives, human and animal, moving across a deadly beautiful northern landscape shot through with permafrost and pocked with muddy depths. Both demand pursuit of mutable forms of sustenance along dually intermittent lines of sight that pass over depths of unknowable threat. Both, in a sense, follow the caribou. Ontological sympathy—alignment, homophony, polyphony—is essential to the perpetuation of both self and other. This is a form of excess that feeds itself. This is a style of being wherever there is a fragment of being. This is meat. This is what they say.

Notes

1 The titular quotation refers to the tracks of a moose (Mandeville 2009, 162). In an earlier translation of the same story cycle, the phrase is rendered, "(This which left these) tracks which we are looking at is meat" (Mandeville 1976, 324).

2 These continuously circulating narratives continue to be instantiated in print. For example, Copper Woman's story, a version of which is the first of Mandeville's stories proper, is extant in the following publications: an

unknown teller to Samuel Hearne in 1771 (published as Hearne 1795); Rabbit's Head to John Franklin in 1820 (Franklin 1823); Ekunelyel to Émile-Fortuné Petitot in 1863 and Alexis Enna-aze to Petitot in 1881 (both published in 1886); Jean Baptiste Ennou to Pliny Earle Goddard in 1911 (Goddard 1912); François Mandeville to Li Fang-Kuei in 1928 (Mandeville 1976, 2009); Joseph Naedzo to June Helm in 1978 (Helm 2000); and Anne Cameron's novel *Daughters of Copper Woman* (1981).

I am grateful to Christopher Cox for telling me about a version of the Copper Woman story recorded in Edward S. Curtis's *The North American Indian* (1928), Volume 18, *The Chipewyan. The Western Woods Cree. The Sarsi*. Titled "Tseqi Tsatsane Hehohl'ai, Woman Copper She-found" (127–28), this version links a wolf guide with caribou food, and it also associates beaver excrement with the appearance of copper.

3 Ronald Scollon and his wife Suzanne Scollon, who did fieldwork in Fort Chipewyan in the 1970s with Mandeville's surviving community and family members (see Scollon and Scollon 1979), were told by Mandeville's son, Philip, that "after hearing many telling of his father's stories as well as the stories of many others over the years, [he] held the view that each storyteller has a different version of a given story, but that each person would have only one of them"; Philip states, "that's the story and that's it: That's the way it goes on right now. A different person tells it and it's all out of shape" (Scollon 2009, 230). Philip's words about his father suggest to me that, in addition to the conversational (one might even call it *polyphonic*) structure identified by Bringhurst, Mandeville's stories extend some of the unique form of his cognitive outlook—a possibility beyond the scope of this chapter, but one that could be pursued in a chapter comparing versions of the same stories told by other people.

4 There are mentions of human flesh—muscle divided from spirit—but always in relation to instances of inter-tribal conflict, and almost never as examples of ingestion, except in one narrative concerning a monstrous but non-human cannibal (story 8, "The Cannibal," Mandeville 2009, 117–24).

5 See, e.g., story 5, "Scabby" (Mandeville 2009, 75–92), in which the protagonist has a pragmatic affinity with rabbits, whose soft fur skins makes it possible for him to manage a potentially debilitating skin condition, and, perhaps as a corollary to wearing their skins, with rabbits as game who

make their bodies abundantly available to his snares when he is tested by his elders.

6 In Li and Scollon's orthography (Mandeville 1976); also spelled, respectively, ʔetthën and -etthën, as in denetthën 'flesh, a person's' (South Slave Divisional Education Council 2012).

7 I am grateful to Leslie Saxon for this insight.

8 In fact, the words for *star, caribou, meat,* and *trail* all come from quite similar places in the mouth: respectively, (ʔe)tthën, ʔɛtθén, ʔɛtθén, ʔetën (South Slave Divisional Education Council 2012). It is not impossible to imagine a cross-linguistic echo in the English word "eatin." In a longer possible "chain or network of metaphorical representations," as Anselmo Urrutia and Joel Sherzer (2000, 147) suggest in their discussion of esoteric lexical associations in Kuna healing songs, these echoes promise to transpose anatomy, to form strange new animals. Stars become meat, tracks become a trail of meaning, innards become skin. Bones rearticulate perpetually to form resolutely historical articulations of Dene truths.

9 In the 1976 translation, the phrase is rendered, "His meat is certainly here again" (Mandeville 1976, 266).

10 In *Ways of Knowing: Experience, Knowledge, and Power among the Dene Tha*, Jean-Guy Goulet (1998, 247) suggests that in a Dene world view "true knowledge is personal knowledge" but also comments on the holistic necessity of narratives as instruments of survival; in order "to apprehend a social world 'as a whole in the form of a personal experience' (Lévi-Strauss 1963, 272) [it] is necessary to depict adequately that world to oneself and to others" (247)—to depict adequately that which is inner as well as outer, both the apparent and the unapparent.

11 There are, by my count, sixteen kinds of animals mentioned at least once in Mandeville's story cycle—bears, wolves, maggots, and puppies among them—and, in future projects, I think it would be fruitful to include the significations of all these animal presences in an intertextual analysis of the story cycle. However, in order to come to understand more fully the metaphysical structures that animals surely embody in Mandeville's narratives, I focus on caribou and moose in this chapter because they are such a common source of sustenance in the stories—and in northern lived experience—and therefore richly embody key cultural domains.

12 I read once that one cannot know the meaning of any story until it is finished; in the case of Mandeville's story cycle, perhaps one cannot know the meaning of any one of the stories without reference to all the others.

13 See especially the formation of a tail of snow when Raven Head runs unnaturally quickly through the snow ahead of his people (Mandeville 2009, 40, 48).

14 "The big fat man leaned down / and put his lips to the man's forehead. / He sucked and drew out blood. / He did the same thing on the back of his head—/ and again he drew out blood. / 'That's why no animals like you,' he said. / 'Now you can make friends.' / The big fat man took him with him / and he opened a doorway in the lick and they went inside" (Ridington and Ridington 2006, 155). A lick is a place in the landscape where mineral salts have naturally accumulated; these deposits draw wild terrestrial ungulates much as a blue salt block in a goat pen draws goats. It seems likely to me that the big fat man is a moose—large and rather jowly as they are—in his human form, which is to say in a form that recognizably signifies personhood to the hunter, but this is conjecture at this point in my research.

15 Likewise, but inversely, for the human who escapes being caribou for the Cannibal.

SECTION THREE

storytelling
to create

CHAPTER SIX

sleepless in Somba K'e

Rita Wong

for the Coney River, otherwise known as the Yellowknife River

twenty thousand people perch on your banks, speaking eleven different languages and more: Chipewyan, Dogrib, Gwich'in, North Slavey, South Slavey, Cree, Inuktitut, Inuvialuktun, Inuinnaqtun, English, French ...

illuminated by the midnight sun, you flow regardless of the Giant Gold Mine and its steady leak of toxins into you, the bustle of unionized Ekati diamond mine workers, the comings & goings of visitors, hunters, bureaucrats, researchers, tourists, more miners, students

Snap Lake is described as "De Beers' first mine outside of Africa," "Canada's first completely underground diamond mine." compared to the gold mines, what legacy will diamond mines leave?

the home of Coney and of Coney-eating Dene for thousands of years, will this short blip of urban disturbance pass as quickly as it began, or will it readjust itself to your rhythms?

what will we learn from crowberry, blueberry, cloudberry, yarrow, caribou, whitefish, Yamozha?

Note
Quotations in this chapter are from De Beers Canada (2015).

CHAPTER SEVEN

Old Rawhide Died

Bren Kolson

Bedtime was another chore defined as work, for my mother.

Yes, it was my father who built the house, the wooden square washstand with stairs my mother climbed in ritual each Monday, to hang clothes on the homemade pulley line. He built the dollhouse beneath the box clothes stand where we played when we were bored with the play-yard, or to cool our bodies and escape the heat on a hot summer's day. He built the garage, sawhorse, and workbenches and the outdoor toilet. He was the master builder, but she was the mistress of all she surveyed. She owned the house, the wood stove, the pots and pans, the three dried raisins at the bottom corner of the hand-built cupboards, the woodpile, the sawdust, switches disguised as willows, the weather, the seasons and time of day.

She owned the in-house café, cooking, brewing, boiling, baking the food and drink for her personal clientele, free of payment and lax of coin as tips. The restaurant was never closed, and customers were never dissuaded from entering to grab a piece of bannock or a drink from *her* cup of tea. She owned and operated the indoor laundromat, where water was dippered one slow drag, one dip at a time, from an aluminum water barrel. Each dipper of water was transferred to large bent cauldrons on the wood stove and, once steamed, was lugged and poured over waiting clothes in the old-fashioned round of the electric wringer-washer.

She was the physician when a child was ill, maintaining a pharmacy of personal choice remedies, mixing Original Peoples' potions and lotions for foreign diseases like chickenpox and measles or crackling unprepared leaves, berries, or what looked like lumps of dirt into boiled water for a cure to drink as tea.

She was the woodcutter, sawing or chopping wood to warm the house to frighten frost when Father was hunting or fishing. She warmed the house as she warmed our hearts. She also warmed the water to wash dirty faces, hands, and feet during weekdays. An aluminum square tub, full of hot water, sitting on two chairs near the glow of embers in the wood stove bought from the Hudson's Bay Company store, was what we dipped our skinny bodies in on Saturday nights.

Saturday night was bath night, when tubs of grey water were hauled outdoors and dumped near the garage as slop water.

Saturday night was quiet time for my mother and father—as were some weeknights when harmony settled the house of loud noises. In flannel two-piece pajamas during winter months, or "whatever you can find to put on" during summer months, we snuggled in our beds, washed and bathed. There were no summer pajamas and no television.

The quarter bed I shared with my sister stayed in a corner through a nearby doorway beside the kitchen. I could see and hear the conversations from my bed, because the rooms were built closely attached. I slept on the side of the bed nearest the kitchen to easily and strategically toss, squirm, and turn to peer over my pillow into the kitchen to see what was happening or to eavesdrop on conversations, especially when the visitors were not of my immediate family's relations.

There was a second reason I wanted to bathe first on Saturday nights, dress in bedtime clothes, and claim the side of the bed next to the kitchen doorway: because I could hear the old brown box radio more clearly there than banked against the wall next to the windy window above our sleep place.

Settling in bed, I would roll over to hug my pillow and watch, through the bars of the brown wrought-iron bed, my mother wiping the floor of spilled wash water, washing the dishes, and placing the eating utensils into cupboards and drawers. I saw her toss towels into the fat bulge of the wringer-washer and rearrange the wood in the box by the wood stove. I knew she knew her domain was intact when she filled the old black kettle with water and I heard the hiss and boil. When she swiped the flowered patterns on the table oilcloth clean of crumbs and spilled or dripped drinks and swept the kitchen floor, the time I waited for was near.

When the work was done, my father would step into the main entryway, or rise from where he napped, to join my mother for tea. I seldom saw my parents drink coffee. If needed and required, the mistress of the house directed her husband to fill the wood-box, take out the slop pail, take out the honey bucket, or go to the porch or garage to bring in a bag of dried meat, dried fish, or a roast of moose or caribou meat for the next day's menu. Once the main chores were done, the children in bed, she kissed each child on the forehead, whether asleep or not, told the ones who were not asleep to "go to sleep now," and went to join her husband at one end of the hand-built kitchen table.

Just before she poured the tea, she did what I waited all week for her to do: Her thumb and forefinger swirled, a quarter-turn, the knob on the old brown box radio.

At a timed second, the radio announcer said: "And Folks! Here's Old Rawhide." Old Rawhide told stories on the radio. His voice sounded like a ninety-nine-year old-timer man who smoked too many uncut tailor-made cigarettes from a green-and-white MacDonald's tin can. The vocal cords quivered, shook as though he was cold and recently came in from a trap-line storm a hundred miles away, somewhere in the freezing night, and never warmed yet. I listened to every sound of Old Rawhide's voice as he told stories about when he was a young man and killed every animal on earth, including grizzly bears, with his bare hands, about the character and homelands of people from lands far away from Yellowknife, Northwest Territories, and stories about a place like New Found Land. At age six, I thought Yellowknife, Northwest Territories, was the only place ever where people lived. The inflections in his voice, precisely pronounced, were enough to force tones of *ooo*, *ahhh*, and *ummmmm* quietly into my pillow of feathers. There was a ritual to my Saturday night. I lived for Saturday nights to listen to Old Rawhide's experiences. He was my hero, who took me to radio places I hoped I would one day see and know.

"Get to sleep," either parent would say from around the corner in the kitchen if I gave myself away by coughing too loud or squirming or wiggling too continuously, by showing signs I was "not about to go to sleep, but still quite awake." My parents wanted quiet in the house when listening to Old Rawhide's Saturday night stories, before the Saturday night hockey game.

Yes, Old Rawhide was my hero. His old, kind, gentle voice—sometimes (well, often times) loud when he talked about ideas that sounded to a child, like "Polly's Ticks" (politics).

The grandfatherly voice informed me of many exciting adventures. I wanted to be just like Old Rawhide when I was his age. I often lay awake before dozing to full sleep, thinking about the stories I heard Old Rawhide tell.

One Saturday in midwinter, the in-house ritual and ceremony of bath night, flannels, and cleanliness was complete. I lay waiting for the sound of the radio button to click. The radio was turned on, but the words from the announcer shocked me into a depressed state of mind.

In as quivering a voice as Old Rawhide, the announcer gave the audience mournful news: "Folks ... we won't be tuning in to Old Rawhide tonight. No, folks, not tonight and not ever again. In fact, we won't ever be listening to Old Rawhide again, folks."

He paused—on the radio—before continuing: "I don't know how to tell you ... and hard for me to say ... but, but, ... Old Rawhide died today. Hard truths, folks, hard for me too, folks. Sorry, folks, I have to go now ... yes, Old Rawhide, a friend of us all, your friend, my friend ... as much a friend of yours as he was of mine ... died ... but I have to go now. One more time, folks, I'm here to tell you of the sad news we won't be hearing Old Rawhide anymore. Old Rawhide died today."

In an un-mourning, professional-radio-sounding voice, he then said: "Now for some uninterrupted classical music." And the music played on.

From my peeping space between the brown wrought-iron bars, I stared wide-eyed at the old brown box radio, shocked at the sad news. Hearing the soulful news Old Rawhide was dead was devastating, but I was indignant when my parents looked at each other, my father saying, "Well. I guess that's that! Have to wait half an hour before the hockey game starts."

There was not so much as a sign or word of condolence about Old Rawhide's death, nor so much as the shedding of a single tear at Old Rawhide's demise. My mom casually picked up a piece of buttered bannock and began chewing slowly. My father whistled a low tune as he refilled the two teacups on the table.

I was shocked, confounded, and soon in a state of depression.

"No more Old Rawhide," I thought. "He's gone. He's gone forever. I'll never hear Old Rawhide's voice again." And, after a respectful moment's silence, came the loud "Waahhhhhhhhhh!" My attempt to cry silently into my feather pillow with my flannel sheet covers pulled over my head, while the other children snored, was to no avail, because I was smothering myself.

When I came up for air, the loud "Wahhhhhh!" shivered my siblings from deep sleep, but no one awoke.

"Whhhaaattt the hell's that kid up to now!" my father said, emphatically and impatiently, at the interruption of my parents' Saturday night quiet time.

"What's wrong," he said, coming to the child sitting in bed sobbing at the loss of a friendly brown box radio voice, crying and crying.

No words could explain the reason I cried. I just cried until he picked me up and rocked me as I spilled raindrop tears on his clean Saturday night hockey shirt shoulder.

"She must have had a bad dream," my mother said from around the corner kitchen wall, where she sat, and I couldn't see her. My father rocked me until the hockey game came on, then laid me on the bed, telling me to go to sleep. The dull lull of the wood stove, the lull-a-bye rocking on my father's shoulder, and exhaustion from crying over Old Rawhide's death was the recipe for sleep.

I walked the wintry play-yard for days, mourning Old Rawhide's death, and in my stupor must have heard, from every person over the age of six, "What's wrong with her? Never seen her so good..." And I never bit the bait, even when my older brothers tried to taunt me into trouble by constantly teasing me.

About two weeks after Old Rawhide's radio death, I was about ready to re-enter society. I knew I could return to my childlike self, half-normal again. I had decided the Saturday night hockey game would never replace Old Rawhide, but would do as an excuse to stay awake longer than my scheduled Saturday night bedtime—when the good news came.

The same Saturday night radio announcer who announced to the world the death of Old Rawhide was now telling the world: "Folks! Good news tonight, folks! We have a surprise for you and a special guest. I'm so pleased to inform you, folks—Old Rawhide's back!"

"Uhhh," I said, gleefully surprised and astonished—as quiet as I could be—when I heard Old Rawhide's voice again: "Folks! I'm back!"

The radio voice was him—Old Rawhide's voice, talking in his old-timer, gruff grandfatherly voice. "No. It's not true what they said about me. Somebody got their shortwave radio wires crossed. I'm back and I'm back to stay. Maybe not forever, but as long as you're listening, folks, I'll be here!"

I was so happy, happy, happy Old Rawhide was back in living flesh—on the radio.

"What happened to her?" my father asked my mother one day as he leaned against her kitchen sink, looking out the kitchen window at the play-yard. "I thought for a while there we were raising the perfect kid. See! See! Look at her! There she goes again! How many times did I tell her to stop throwing sawdust at the poor dog."

My mother leaned toward the window, over the kitchen counter, surveying the yard. She looked at my father, and my parents stood staring face-to-face, sipping tea, waiting to see who would break the stare and silence to say something about who would first reveal parenting skills about "tthhhaaat kid."

Note

Bren Kolson's story "Old Rawhide Died" is based on the true radio voice characters of Max Ferguson, who died on 7 March 2013. A short biography of Max Ferguson, detailing his career in broadcasting, is available from CBC News at http://www.cbc.ca/news/entertainment/cbc-radio-s-max-ferguson-dies-1.1414648.

CHAPTER EIGHT

Métis Storytelling across Time and Space: Situating the Personal and Academic Self Between Homelands

Zoe Todd

Introduction

I moved to perpetually grey Aberdeen, Scotland, in September 2010. I packed up all my things, gave away boxes and boxes of books and clothes, stopped briefly in Halifax to visit a nicimos (sweetheart), and finally crossed the threshold of the Atlantic to launch into a PhD in anthropology.

At home, on the prairies, my family's stories are woven into the landscape. The saskatoons that flourish in the river valley every July hold memories of stories shared by my dad when I was young. The patches of grass and pillars of concrete that stand where my dad's grandparents lived in **pêhonân** offer at least a small testimony to the places where people before me lived out the movements and moments of their lives. But how do we connect to time and history when we are *away* from our homeland? How can an Indigenous person make sense of self and of political, cultural, economic, and social realities while living on the other side of the world? Can one generate *Indigenous* stories while living in the heart of the former colonial empire? And how can storytelling generate meaningful research relationships when working "away from home"?

In this chapter I offer a creative investigation of my own application of "Indigenous Métissage" (Donald 2012) as I split my life between the prairies, the Canadian Arctic, and Scotland. I demonstrate how I use storytelling, poetry, and creative non-fiction to engage in complex conversations about responsibilities and reciprocity. I also illustrate how storytelling became an integral part of my research methodology and scholarship as I worked within the context of different Indigenous homelands.

I will begin with a story:

In summer the berries ripen
Deep purple

We drive and drive and drive
In the melt-through-glass heat
Legs stuck to vinyl seats
The stale smell of cigarettes and dirt
And years on the highway

Through parts of town where houses have windows
Smashed in by bats
Not balls

We move furniture for women
Kicked out by yet another slimy landlord
Sister and I play with kids as their toys are loaded up onto the truck
Eat gum
Spit it out
You can't get that Beemans anymore
Sometimes we race up the stairs ahead of the beds and chairs
Dazzled by the late-day, end-of-the-month sun

Hop up onto the empty truck bed
Order sister around
Let's put that dresser over here
And move that table
No good falling over fool

I figure everyone lives in apartments
If they are young
I figure it's normal to move every month or so
To have a man with bad breath hand you keys
Glance at you sideways

Dad says he's glad he was there
"did you see that bastard?"
I think bastards are the people who give you keys to apartments

When the end of the month passes
The truck goes back to being just a plain old truck
For riding around
For swearing at no-good jerks who cut us off
For hauling things from dumpsters
Much to mom's chagrin

But it's in the summer
When the berries ripen
That we drive down Keillor Road
And dad points out the women
With pails
Picking Saskatoon berries

Look—he says—
Those women picked those berries
As long as I can remember

I think back to the day before
That's as far as I can remember
That's a long time

These women picked these berries for a long time
Today when I run down the crumbling road
That used to lead us past the women

I see no one

And I realize
I didn't ask them
where to find the best berries

I find myself alone, here, in this foreign Scottish city. Just me and the sound of cars driving slowly down our street, the windows open to the mild warmth gracing the trees, the grass, the granite buildings. Despite its best efforts, the sun can't penetrate the stucco and stone walls of my flat, so it is perpetually chilly inside. I drink my coffee meditatively, closing my eyes and allowing the fresh aroma to drift to my nose. I breathe in deeply, try to relax. With my eyes closed, I feel my body and my spirit drifting between here and home. I am perpetually in-between. Somewhere out there is the North Sea, the same sea that those Hudson's Bay boys plied all those years ago on their way to Canada. And although my great-great-great-great-grandfather, William Ernest Todd, was born in Dublin, I still like to imagine that at least once—maybe when he was still in the Royal Navy—he stared out at these same frigid waters and wondered what life across the Atlantic would bring.

I know him through paper: articles written by the meticulous historian Arthur Ray, who was as spellbound by my ancestor's character and wit as I am today. I pull out the notes I took from William's journal, from the stuffy June 2010 day I spent holed up inside the Hudson's Bay Archives in Winnipeg. As the large grandfather clock in the centre of the archives ticked quietly, and the silence was broken every so often by an anonymous cough or the clearing of a throat, I carefully turned those fragile pages covered in his masterful penmanship, and I drank in his words. With each page, I felt like I was reaching back through time, listening to him tell his stories as though we were sitting in the same room. As I look at my notes today, I try to imagine what it was like for him to travel the seas all those times, back and forth between the Americas and Britain. I can barely bring myself to board a plane, seized as I am by terror at the thought of its sailing down into the dark, unforgiving waters. But he boarded those ships again and again. Built a life across the ocean, married, had children. Fought with politicians, stood his ground.

My thoughts turn to my Métis great-great-great-great-grandmothers—the texts are unclear on which of William's wives gave birth to my direct ancestor, William Todd II. William's first wife was Marianne Ballentyne, and his second wife was Isabella Elizabeth Dennet. They who are silent. The textual record cannot even agree on who they gave birth to! No written journals, no letters or songs. I like to imagine that my feistiness, the fire that burns bright in my heart, is from them and from my other Todd women relatives, at least in part. Marianne and Isabella—they raised the children. They joined their husband as he moved across the country working for the Hudson's Bay Company. They died before him, leaving a legacy of children who went on to live throughout many parts of the prairies (like so many Métis families). Cousins spread far and wide between northern British Columbia and the Red River. I wish I could hold, even for a fleeting second, something that Marianne or Isabella had touched or made. I think of the people who fly across the waters to reclaim artefacts from musty museum storage rooms. Wouldn't it be wonderful if someone had saved Todd women's handiwork? But maybe it would be heartbreaking to fight with well-meaning bureaucrats just to get a glimpse of your own family's legacy. So I tuck away the thought, grateful that we have access to the journals.

The same summer that I trekked to the archives, I also sought out our family "homeland." When my cousin and I stood on what remains of the land William was given in 1850 by the Hudson's Bay Company along the Assiniboine River, in St. James, it felt as though time stood still. Across the river, the joyous shouts of children and families enjoying a sunny afternoon at Assiniboine Park emanated from the trees. There was nary a building in sight, and for a very brief moment I imagined it was 1850, and I was there with my ancestors, on the precipice of the acute pain and struggle they and other Métis would face in the years to come as intense colonial settlement shifted relationships and governance across the prairies.

Just a year after he was given that land, William Todd would be dead. And in twenty years the Red River Métis would fight for recognition of their rights in the place they had lived all their lives. A part of me wishes William had lived long enough to be there for the resistances. In 1837, when he was stationed as Chief Trader at Fort Pelly, he heard from men he was trading with that Fort Union in the United States of America had closed its doors. He was troubled by the accounts of a sickness afflicting the Fort, and asked the men for as much detail as possible. He suspected smallpox. He fretted and worried. What would this mean for the Cree and Assiniboine he traded with? Would they survive the outbreak if it snaked its way north of the border? Could he live with himself knowing that innocent people were dying? People were still suspicious of vaccines. Did they really work? No one had tried them out west yet. He collected as many company-issue vaccines as he could. He cursed the defective ones. He tried to warn other traders and factors. He taught the chiefs who came to the Fort how to inoculate their families back at their camps. He used every tool in his arsenal to stop the outbreak in its tracks. Through a tense winter, he worried about whether he had been right. And in the melting spring, he was relieved to learn from visiting chiefs and their parties that he had been right: the sickness had come, but those who had been inoculated were spared.

You would think that such actions would bring recognition, or at least thanks, from the shrewd businessmen of the HBC. However, my great-great-great-great-grandfather had earned the scorn of Governor Simpson—who had once considered him the top surgeon in the west—for being a stubborn, lively man. He would go on to die somewhat broken, fighting unsuccessfully for the HBC to promote him to Factor to the very end.

It is strange to feel so connected to someone I have never met. But his story and his ferocity inspire me. The complexity of my roots remains: Métis, nêhiyaw, Scots-Irish, French, German, Norwegian, English. And I cannot tell the full story of my family and our responsibilities by relying solely on Dr. Todd's generation. There are many more kinship obligations and narratives woven into our family's history as my ancestors moved through the Lake Winnipeg watershed throughout the nineteenth and twentieth centuries. I can't claim connection to a single moment in time, but I can ponder how my own ancestors lived out their lives according to their principles. How they negotiated their responsibilities in relation to the people—human and more-than-human—with whom they shared time and place. I want to honour William's legacy. I want to honour the legacy of my aunties, uncles, grandparents, great-grandparents. Whatever it was that William and Marianne and Isabella had, something deep inside them that guided them through incredible events.

It is easy to feel alone over here, across the gaping ocean. I try to see myself and my family reflected in the faces I pass on the street. I hear echoes of my ancestry in the fiddle music, the dance, the bannock and tea. I feel home but not home. It is a strange, visceral feeling. It is as if I knew this place before I was born, and yet it still feels so foreign. My heart aches for open prairie fields, dusty train tracks and grain elevators, saskatoons and coyote calls.

I get up from my desk. The coffee is cold now. The sun is blazing through my window, washing the room in bright, effortless light. I grab my coat, plug in my earphones, and set out into the street. I wind my way through the medieval buildings of Old Aberdeen. I pass Old King's College, the squat Town Square. I listen to the thup-thup-thup of cars driving too fast on the narrow cobblestone road. I make my way to an intersection and wait for the interminable light to switch to green so that I can cross. Cars whiz by, and when I glance to my right I can see the sea stretching out on the horizon, fishing trawlers bobbing in the liquid golden sunlight.

As I cross the street, I am suddenly seized by a desire to walk through the botanical gardens to my left. I enter the gates of the garden and saunter past the research building. As I round a corner, I stop in my tracks. There, in the late-day sun, stands a saskatoon bush. I rub my eyes, incredulous. How? How could there be saskatoons in Aberdeen? I walk up to the plant slowly, carefully. I eye the plant up close, instantly recognizing the plump, dusty, purple-blue skin and jagged, rounded leaves. It's a saskatoon, all right. I almost laugh out loud, wanting to hug this plant. Months of worry and loneliness wash out of my body as I remember years and years of picking berries in the North Saskatchewan River Valley with friends. Every July I scoped out the richest, ripest spots and filled buckets with saskatoons that I ate in the autumn. For a moment I am transported back home, to the melt-through-glass heat of an Alberta summer.

I start to eagerly imagine all the pies, tarts, jams, and shortcakes I could make with these berries if I could find a way to sneak them out of the garden. And in this hazy evening, with the sun slung low between the trees, I feel between places. I feel home. I know I can't harvest buckets of berries from this prim botanical garden, but I can sneak one or two saskatoons from the branches while no one is looking. I raise the delicate berries to the sun, saluting my good fortune.

...

A few years later, as I write up my dissertation from a mouldy little room in Dundee, I return to the Aberdeen botanical garden with my friend Lou. Emboldened by a few years of refusal of British politesse, no longer scared to flout British social norms, I take my dear friend on an excursion to harvest berries from the prim university botanical gardens. As we pick berries and fill our Tupperware containers, giggling and laughing as graduate students and garden technicians walk by, I feel a delicious kind of transcendence. It is not just the sweetness of the berry that gives me pleasure, but also the fleshy presence of my large and unapologetic Métis body picking these berries and tending to them, both of us—plant and human—transplanted so far from the prairies we thirst for. I tell Lou stories about wooing many a nicimos in Edmonton by taking them to my favourite saskatoon-picking spots on the banks of the North Saskatchewan. She and I laugh, and I feel a kind of hope and kinship here, with my Yorkshire friend, who later reciprocates this excursion by taking me to the west coast and showing me the stunning landscapes of the Scottish Highlands.

Between time and space, I find hope in the dusty purple flesh of misâsk-watômina. And I think of that transported saskatoon bush often, tending as it is to *a complex history of botanical colonialism—defiantly flowering every spring and yielding its rich blue-purple fruit every July while Brits walk by, unaware of the rich stories teasing them from the green.*

In the summer, the berries ripen: I eat these in honour of you, all my Todd relations who moved through those dusty prairie summers with grace and determination.

First, to contextualize this story: I wrote the first draft of this piece about saskatoons from a spare bedroom in a friend's house in Paulatuuq, Northwest Territories, in the spring of 2012. I was conducting PhD research on fishing in this small coastal Inuvialuit hamlet of 350 residents, and found myself with lots of time to write and reflect on my experiences as an Indigenous woman working across spatial, cultural and political boundaries. While filleted char and butchered caribou sat quietly in the freezer humming next to me, I sat on my bed with a cup of coffee and decided to write out the story of how I came to discover a lone Saskatoon bush—misâskwatômina—on the University of Aberdeen campus. My piece did not capture the attention of the writing-contest jury that I submitted it to, but it did allow me to interrogate my own feelings of being simultaneously at home and away, feelings that were very keen as I worked in the small Arctic hamlet. I began to realize that I often find myself *in-between* geographical and temporal spaces. I am forced, through circumstances and through relationships I develop in my work and my personal life, to employ Indigenous Métissage (Donald 2012, 534) as I make sense of how to *be* Indigenous while moving through the world. Stories and storytelling, and the ways in which they are woven into many disparate landscapes, have become a central part of how I situate and express myself within my academic life in Scotland, my research life in the Arctic, and my personal and political life in Edmonton, Alberta (amiskwaciwâskahikan).

Now, to contextualize the theoretical portion of this chapter: I wrote the first draft of this theoretical piece on reciprocity, research, and storytelling in November 2013, expanding on the story I wrote in Paulatuuq in the spring of 2012. I am returning to it, more than three years later, to make it as accountable and honest as possible. I strive here, in this circular return to the text, to tell the best stories. I therefore endeavour, in this final version, to reflect the temporal and geographic journey the multiple iterations and refracturings that the stories shared in this piece have undergone. Before I demonstrate the role of storytelling in my work, it is important to situate this piece within broader anthropological thinking on storytelling. There is an incredibly rich anthropological literature on the use of stories and their importance. As Michael Jackson ([2002] 2006, 12) notes, storytelling is a powerful way to examine the "relationship between microcosm and macrocosm, thereby embracing the relationship between the visible and the invisible, the familiar and the foreign, and the living and the dead." In other words, stories are valuable. Stories carry meaning. And stories are relational—both in the creation and in the telling. The performance of stories is also as vital as the texts that they contain. We cannot break them down solely to the words written on a page; rather, we must hold the entire performance and existence of a story to our hearts as we try to understand what it is the storyteller is communicating to their chosen audience. Dell Hymes (2003, 72) urges us to remember that

> fieldwork with ongoing traditions is vital. Documentation of living performance is absorbing, but reading matters too. It is the way we can recreate something of the imaginative world, the intertextuality, in which a given telling arose and so recognize and appreciate a teller's aesthetic and moral imagination. If all one has is the one occasion, one may miss important aspects of what is there. Narrators create in performances but also between performances. *Stories are good to hear, but also good to think.* (emphasis added)

Stories are a method, in their own right, and a rigorous one at that. The creation, performance, re-narration, and sharing of stories provide opportunities for both researcher and participant to deconstruct and recalibrate experience and knowledge. In the anthropological research context, stories and conversations also bind us in relationships that endure over time (Cruikshank 1998, 25). Textual and performative aspects of storytelling hold clues that we must heed in order to situate ourselves in *place*.

As I pursued my PhD, I split my time between Aberdeen, Scotland; Edmonton, Alberta; and Paulatuuq, Northwest Territories, for the better part of three years. In all of that motion, I felt as though I embodied the movement and persistence of my Métis ancestors. Though I was not *on* or *in* the traditional territory of my family for most of the year, I carried a part of them with me everywhere I went. Some Indigenous scholars argue that the resurgence of Indigenous peoples is contingent upon reconnecting to our homelands (Alfred and Corntassel 2005), but for some of us the physical reconnection to land is patently impossible. For the Métis—themselves forced into movement across western Canada—this becomes an incredibly challenging and fraught prospect.

Is it possible, then, for the Métis scholar, to incorporate connections to land, memory, language, and identity into one's work while also *moving across* homelands and disciplines? Through choosing to work and study in the United Kingdom, I bring the experiences of my Scottish-Métis ancestors to Scotland to "speak back to Empire" (Brennan 2001, 92), in my own small way. In order to stay grounded and remain connected to my family, my community, and my sense of self as a Métis woman, I employ storytelling and art as a way to reassert my place in the world, and to remind those in the home of colonial actors like John A. Macdonald that we still exist. We live, breathe, think, love, and move through the world to this very day. By working in the Northwest Territories, I am faced with questions of what it means to be Indigenous and work within another Indigenous people's homeland, of how to develop meaningful and respectful relationships within various social, cultural, and political contexts. In all of these cases—at home, in Scotland, and in the Arctic—storytelling becomes a powerful and effective way to confront and make meaning of my situation and role as an Indigenous scholar, community member, and woman. Through the serious labour that stories do, I try to embody my ongoing responsibilities as a philosopher, researcher, and interlocutor in relational ways across multiple spatial and temporal terrains.

Bringing "Place" and Identity into Scholarship through Storytelling

The central conundrum of remaining connected to place and a strong sense of self while also moving between territories and disciplines is not easy to resolve. My approach to the challenges of movement, identity, and work is to employ a bit of subversion. As a white-coded Métis woman, I must also account for my white privilege and all that it affords me as I move through academic and non-academic spaces. This creates a deep responsibility to refuse white supremacy when it manifests within academia and beyond, and to vociferously challenge ongoing colonial thinking which informs many aspects of the academy writ large. One thing I have learned over the years is that working in the field of anthropology opens up many opportunities to be spoken *to* about Indigeneity by white scholars, which is itself a deeply *non-reciprocal* experience of Indigeneity within the discipline. However, working within this discipline also allows for professional encounters in which oral history and stories are afforded value. By bringing my own suitcase full of stories from home, I challenge and subvert ideas about Indigeneity as they emerge in popular culture and academic spaces in Britain. However, because I work *as* an anthropologist, assumptions are often made about my affiliations and relationships: I am very often situated as the exploitive white researcher—and rightly so, given the epistemic violence inherent in the history of the discipline (Simpson 2014, 95–114) and related fields such as geography (Hunt 2014, 29). As Simpson (2014, 95) states, "to speak of Indigeneity is to speak of colonialism and anthropology." The idea that anthropology is intimately connected to processes of colonization (Simpson 2007, 2014) requires that Indigenous anthropologists situate and explain their own relationships to the discipline today, and that we strive not to recreate the exploitative structures that the discipline mobilized and reproduced in the past (and still reproduces today). It requires an honest positioning within the ongoing realities of the academy, and of anthropology, as "white public space" (Brodkin, Morgen, and Hutchinson 2011), and a willingness to directly and forthrightly trouble and unsettle understandings of how Indigenous philosophies and methodologies manifest and are mobilized by Indigenous peoples.

As a result of the many competing challenges of relationship, movement, and identity for the Indigenous scholar working away from home, working between non-Indigenous and Indigenous spaces creates complex moments in the research relationship. Nonetheless, it also affords particular experiences that are not possible if we refuse to work across difference (Donald 2012). It is during moments of confrontation, both in the field and in the academy— the moments of confusion about who I am—that storytelling becomes a powerful way to explain where I come from and what I stand for. Through storytelling, I bring the experiences of my life so intimately rooted in the place of my childhood, amiskwaciwâskahikan, directly into relation with friends and colleagues in Scotland and Paulatuuq. Place, kinship, identity, and memory are thus evoked and enlivened as I bring them into conversations with other actors through the telling of stories.

The use of stories is not always smooth or without conflict. Confrontation is a transformative tool which Métis scholar and artist David Garneau urges scholars to employ in his powerful perspective on the notion of working within anthropology. In a discussion in the (now defunct) Metis Studies Facebook group in January 2012, I voiced my frustration over the disconnect I felt between the discourses I was engaging in in Indigenous circles in Canada and the perceptions I had of my duties as an anthropologist. Expressing disbelief at my resigned conclusion that it was not possible to engage in anthropology as an Indigenous person without compromising my identity and integrity, Garneau instead suggested that

> Being Métis can be (re)constructed by your practice neither as a discourse of victimhood and survival or as a colonial agent, but as a free-trader whose agenda (trading) is known to those with whom you hope to trade. The question becomes, what are you sharing? What do you have that is of perceived equal value to those with whom you hope to do exchange?
>
> The secret purpose of any institution (including Anthropology and anthropology students) is to know itself through confrontation with others. If you do in fact have an essential difference from the institution it will be borne out in your encounter with it. If it is genuine, it will survive the relationship and both will be altered. (David Garneau, personal communication, 2012)

Reflecting Garneau's thoughts, my research in Paulatuuq relied heavily on my relationships with community members. These relationships evolved from the confrontation of me as anthropologist–outsider with local day-to-day life of Paulatuuqmiut (Paulatuuq people). Despite my best efforts to be either the very best *Indigenous* researcher or the very best *anthropological* researcher possible, the reality is that my lived experiences as a Métis intellectual are shaped by Garneau's principle of "thought-trading," which entails negotiating sameness and difference both in the classroom and in the field. In this way, stories and storytelling, art and creative expression, played a crucial role in my ability to articulate identity, relationships, responsibilities, and my shifting position as scholar, traveller, and political agent as I moved between Scotland, the prairies, and the Northwest Territories.

Storytelling enabled a form of reciprocal engagement with people and place in the three places among which I split my life during my PhD. Storytelling was also a way to create a sense of vulnerability and trust that is otherwise difficult to achieve in the top-down power dynamics of "official" research methodologies, such as interviews, surveys, and workshops. Without meaning to sound romantic, storytelling opened up a much more reciprocal space. In this reciprocal space, friends and I shared stories, jokes, anecdotes, and memories. These were also the spaces where I was questioned firmly about my work, guided towards different ways of approaching things, and held reciprocally responsible for my actions. These reciprocal moments were shared while drinking cups of tea, while travelling on the land, and while waiting out days when we were weathered in by the infamous Paulatuuq South Wind. As a Métis researcher, I was embedded within systems both within the discipline of anthropology and within the legal–governance frameworks employed in Paulatuuq, which necessitated a relational approach and which brought my stories from the prairies directly into intimate contexts of research, friendship, accountability, narrative, and working across difference.

Towards a Métis Methodology: Storytelling as Research Practice
What my time in anthropology and my movement between home and away have revealed, very quickly, is the paucity of theory around the practice of anthropology from a Métis perspective. There is very important literature that addresses Indigenous engagement with anthropology, such as Simpson's "ethnographic refusal" (Simpson 2007), wherein Indigenous peoples can destabilize the research process by refusing to share that which could harm Indigenous nationhood and sovereignty. Beatrice Medicine's work investigates the role of the Indigenous person as anthropologist, arguing that Indigenous anthropologists offer a crucial and unique perspective and can play a transformative role in the discipline (Medicine and Jacobs 2001). However, little work deals directly with Métis methodologies of anthropology. I seek here to offer a tentative framework for an emerging "Métis methodology" in the practice of anthropology.

In light of the lack of work dealing with Métis methods, or with the position of the Métis researcher within the discipline of anthropology, I find Dwayne Donald's work on "Indigenous Métissage" (Donald 2012, 534) incredibly instructive. As Donald writes,

> My particular problem, in terms of identity and belonging, is that I have been
> led to believe that I cannot live my life as though I am both an Aboriginal

person and the grandson of European settlers. As a citizen and aspiring academic, there has been considerable pressure to choose sides, to choose a life
inside or outside the walls of the fort (Donald 2009a). (Donald 2012, 534)

Both Donald and Garneau reiterate the significance of working across
experiences, relationships, and histories with care. One of the challenges
of existing methodological work is that it forces those who find themselves
working within complex spaces to employ overly simplistic or polarized
notions to explain their relationships to place, people, and politics, rather
than taking a more relational view of how these interactions unfold over time
(Donald 2012). Existing Indigenous research methodologies enabled me to
interrogate my relationship to both Paulatuuqmiut *and* anthropology, but I
too felt the pressure to "choose sides," as Donald describes. It was moments
of unexpected storytelling that often challenged the dualities that emerge in
academic and political discourses of working within Indigenous contexts,
and thus it was the sharing of stories that allowed a different set of research
relationships—and responsibilities—to emerge.

Evans et al. (2012) detail the ethical principles that researchers and community members should follow in enacting Métis health research. I look
to these as useful in trying to articulate a "Métis methodology" within disciplines like Anthropology. Evans et al.'s principles are informed by broader
Indigenous methodological discourse but are also unique to Métis practices and knowledge. One of the principles they identify as crucial to Métis
research is *reciprocity*, summarized in plain-language materials distributed by
the National Aboriginal Health Organization as follows:

> By reciprocity it was meant that there would be equal partnerships, *which*
> *includes equal responsibility and equal benefits.* Also, there was the explicit expec-
> tation that all involved would learn from each other. (National Aboriginal
> Health Organization 2010, 2; emphasis added)

The notions of equal responsibility and equal benefits are useful in framing an effective "Métis" methodology of anthropology. Reciprocity also
enlivens the space outlined and framed by Donald's "Indigenous Métissage"
and Garneau's "thought-trading." In this case, we need a more nuanced and
responsive understanding of Indigenous spaces as *diverse* and *complex*,

and we need not to deny Indigenous peoples the same agency we extend to other actors. We must situate our research within broader historical contexts of colonialism and state activities. We must also acknowledge those voices within Indigenous spaces that are marginalized, and in fact silenced, within existing political and research frameworks. Research methodologies must acknowledge that Indigenous people are not uniform instead diverse and heterogeneous (Evans et al. 2012). As academics, we must query how our position as researchers intersects with various local politics and power dynamics, and acknowledge the sometimes invisible ways in which power is mobilized—as Steven Lukes ([1974] 2005, 64) argues in his seminal 1974 piece on the three dimensions of power, power "is at its most effective when least accessible to observation, to actors and observers alike" (64). By ignoring the ways in which power circulates within Indigenous spaces, researchers and research bodies risk being complicit in structures that silence or harm those they seek to protect through contemporary ethics processes. Responsive research should be aware of—and sensitive to—local and regional political and power structures, and understand how the project of research is affected by these relationships. I found, anecdotally, that stories and storytelling were an effective and affective way to mobilize reciprocal learning and partnership, to explain my situation as an Indigenous person within a broader non-Indigenous discipline, and to create safer spaces for others to approach me about why I was doing the work I was, and offer their own thoughts on how to make the work better, how to be more responsive to the community, and how to better reflect people's *own* stories.

Storytelling was a creative way to quietly engage outside of formal, top-down research frameworks. People chose when and where they shared stories with me—often to offer a lesson or an explanation of life within the community that challenged outside perceptions of community dynamics. Storytelling also enabled those who might not be considered official holders of knowledge by those in power within the community to impart their own knowledge outside of boardrooms. Stories emerged in line at the grocery store, while stopping to chat on the road, while drinking a cup of coffee out at fish camp. Stories were also shared in the form of songs and jam sessions at the local radio station, or while visiting Elders for tea. Stories did not require the formalized rubrics of university-sanctioned surveys or workshops. Stories were also co-created through relationships and shared experiences. I still remember, in the midst of getting lost on our way back to town from a fishing trip to Thrasher Lake without any Elders to guide us, how my friend Lanita turned around while driving the all-terrain vehicle and said, "Please tell me this story is going in your study!" I laughed, because it really was a good story—three women managing to navigate the landscape before the September sunset, getting stuck in various mud pits, keeping an eye out for aklak (grizzlies) and tuktu (caribou), but thankfully remembering to orient ourselves towards the coast to the north so that we could eventually follow the ocean back to town.

Reciprocity is not exclusive to Métis research, by any means. It is very important for scholars to acknowledge and understand the ways in which some researchers take without giving to Indigenous peoples with whom they work. Linda Tuhiwai Smith (1999) wrote seminal work on challenging the exploitative dynamics of research in Indigenous communities in New Zealand, arguing powerfully for a mobilization of decolonizing methodologies which refuse the logics and processes of colonial institutions and powers. With her work in mind, I believe we must also explore the complex relationships that emerge throughout the process of anthropological inquiry. Murielle Nagy (2012) offers a good investigation of how reciprocal relationships can be mobilized in the conduct and dissemination of research within Indigenous communities. She details a cogent exploration of the shared nature of research processes and products, and queries some of the challenges that may arise once a project is finished. Who owns the written reports once a collaborative project is done? Should researchers have access to data they have collected once a contract is finished? How do reciprocal relationships emerge in the process of collaborative work? These are issues that the field of Arctic anthropology continues to grapple with. For these reasons, questions of intellectual property rights and reciprocity deserve a fuller, more complex treatment in the literature than we have given them to date. These are by no means new questions; rather, they are a re-articulation of ongoing labour that Indigenous peoples assert in dynamic contexts through time and space to decolonize research methodologies and assert reciprocal responsibilities between parties. Taking such an approach will enable us to address the relational aspect of research more accurately and to develop transparent and respectful ways of approaching the praxis and production of research. I argue that by framing work around Donald's notion of Indigenous Métissage, we can work through the relational aspects of research more fully.

Reciprocity is a familiar theme in anthropology, as James Clifford (1980) demonstrates in his examination of the role of reciprocity in anthropologist Maurice Leenhardt's work. Clifford (2004) also discusses the existence of reciprocity in anthropological work in Indigenous contexts over time. I argue that a renewed focus on reciprocal responsibilities creates discursive space to foster respectful working research relationships in Indigenous contexts in Canada. The relational and accountable research methods that Indigenous scholars such as Shawn Wilson (2008, 80–96, 97–125) argue for, such as approaching "research as ceremony," are instructive, and storytelling is one way in which meanings and understandings can be offered, critiqued, shifted, and re-narrated. Storytelling can also enable confrontational or provocative information to be shared in a contextual manner, providing the nuance and meaning so easily lost in sanitized surveys or rushed interviews. In my experience working in Paulatuuq and in Scotland, stories emerge on their own terms, when the people who choose to share them want to share them. They may emerge at unexpected moments, and may reverberate and shift over time. Stories, in a way, have a life of their own, and they bind people who both give and receive them in relationships that transcend spatiotemporal boundaries (Cruikshank 1998, 25).

Conclusion

Storytelling is a tool that I employ, in my research and in my day-to-day life, to situate myself amidst shifting homelands and to evoke my prairie-life wherever I find myself. It is a way to explain my relationship to anthropology and also to the places in which I work. Stories are also a way to subvert and challenge top-down research relationships that tend to marginalize or silence those who do not hold the balance of power in particular contexts. By using stories and storytelling, I try to honour Donald's notion of Indigenous Métissage—creating space to "hold together the ambiguous, layered, complex, and conflictual character of Aboriginal and Canadian relations without the need to deny, assimilate, hybridize or conclude" (Donald 2012, 536). In using stories as I navigate the circuitous path of academia—and while I work in the homelands of other Indigenous peoples—I try to unambiguously explain who I am, where I come from, what I have to "offer" (Garneau, personal communication, 2012), and engage my reciprocal responsibilities to those with whom I work with a great deal of care.

In the absence of a comprehensive "Métis methodology" for the practice of anthropology, storytelling can be one way to inhabit Garneau's thought-trader persona and Donald's Indigenous Métissage framework and to offer something reciprocal and accountable to those with whom we work. Stories are also a way to ensure that information is shared more immediately and more transparently. The relationships that emerge through the use of stories and storytelling can provide a counter-narrative to the either/or discourses that currently dominate many academic and political contexts. We have the tools, now, to inhabit a reciprocal, relational space that honours our differences and is cognizant of broader political and historical realities and structural power imbalances while also striving to ensure that the stories erased by those in power are heard.

In the summer the berries ripen …

Conclusion

Julia Christensen, Christopher Cox, and Lisa Szabo-Jones

The stories in this collection have travelled away from that warm, sunny week on Yellowknives Dene First Nation territory, from cluttered desks and kitchen tables, to take up space here on these pages. They have also travelled in the sense that their purpose and contribution have evolved through the coming together of these chapters and the dialogue and cross-fertilization that have materialized between them. The original intent of this collection was to explore storytelling as a mode of understanding, sharing, and creating knowledge by collectively asking how storytelling advances responsible citizenship and human relationships with the natural environment at the local, national, and global levels. The chapters speak to one another to reveal a meaningful interdisciplinary and cross-cultural dialogue with important insights in terms of policy-making, activism, meaning, and healing. What has come out of them is not a singular or formulaic approach but, rather, a recognition of the diversity of forms that storytelling can take, as well as the multiplicity of its objectives and outcomes. Across the chapters, two main themes emerge: first, storytelling as an approach to knowledge sharing, in terms both of its capacity as a methodology and its role in sharing knowledge with wider audiences; and, second, storytelling as a political and epistemological act in taking back space for Indigenous ways of knowing (and at the same time creating new spaces for other culturally embedded ways of knowing within the Eurocentric academy). Together, these themes point to the enduring, ever-evolving significance of Métis scholar and activist Jo-Ann Episkenew's (2009) writing on the power(s) of Indigenous stories and storytelling. Reflecting the spirit captured in Episkenew's work, the chapters in this collection showcase stories not only as a means to understand the power imbalances between European and Indigenous forms of knowledge within academia but also as narrative, discursive, and even material spaces through which healing may be activated.

Storytelling as a Methodology

All of the chapters in this collection go beyond storytelling as method to employ storytelling as a methodology in various ways. That is to say, for the contributors to this book, storytelling is more than a research tool: it is a spirit through which one engages with knowledge, its holders, and the places in which it sits. For Sandercock and Todd, storytelling acts as a form of inquiry, a way to interrogate both the field or topic of research and the self as researcher/storyteller. Rather than employ a writing style conventional to western academia, both find freedom in telling stories that examine the ways in which their personal, emotional geographies have shaped and challenged their engagements as academics. What's more, storytelling becomes a way of holding oneself accountable in describing and analyzing one's experiences and observations. The distancing often found in conventional academic writing—for instance, employing the third person and the passive voice—becomes impossible in the kinds of writing in which Sandercock and Todd engage. Their selves are made visible, even vulnerable, as they explore their own interventions and interactions within a field.

For Todd, her positionality as an Indigenous woman working within and across Indigenous homelands frames a sense of responsibility and reciprocity that knows no professional or disciplinary bounds. The necessarily complex analysis of this positionality and its effects and affects is made possible by her engagements with creative writing, in part because these forms of storytelling allow her to transcend time and space to consider the kinship obligations and narratives woven into her family's history. In her chapter, saskatoon berries, and the juxtaposed images of them growing wild on their native prairies and then as a transplanted specimen of the "new world" brought back to Scotland, become a material representation of this transcendence. Moreover, the narrative Todd constructs in this chapter allows her to expose herself as a scholar working through the often messy and scattered process of writing. The transcendence of time and space is also invoked in how she reveals the backdrop to her story of saskatoon berries, working various pieces into a patchwork of inquiry and exploration that spans the beginning of her doctoral studies in Aberdeen, then Paulatuuq, then Edmonton, and places in between, and finally to Ottawa, where, as a newly minted assistant professor, she rewrote this piece into its final version. Storytelling is thus not just a methodology for the creation, performance, or sharing of stories but it is also political. For, as Todd elaborates, as a Métis scholar, carrying of stories across time and space—a process embodied here not only by Todd herself but by the wild persistence of the saskatoon berries—becomes not only a form of knowledge sharing but also a taking-up of space within the western academy, across Eurocentric disciplinary bounds, between homelands. Storytelling also challenges conventional methodological approaches, which require the researcher to choose sides, and instead takes on a more relational view of how interactions between places, peoples, and politics unfold over time. In this way, storytelling enables Todd to interrogate the diverse and shifting relations she encountered with places and peoples, as well as with the discipline within which she is situated in western academia: anthropology.

For Sandercock, storytelling as inquiry enables important methodological engagements with reflexivity. In her chapter, she asks herself how her work in Burns Lake was not only transformative for the community with whom she worked but also for herself as a non-Indigenous scholar. To begin, she takes a long and difficult look at the structures of the planning paradigms within which her work is unavoidably situated. In particular, she asks herself how the history of planning as a discipline and practice is part and parcel of the very colonial and modernist systems she seeks to dismantle and resist in her work. Sandercock uncovers the myriad ways in which planning produces and performs stories of its own, through its bylaws, blueprints, disciplinary rhetoric, and technologies of power, all of which play distinct roles in reproducing the colonial present. Her poem allows her to confront this weighted past and present and what they mean for her own practice and identity as a planner. Is there a way, she asks, for planning to engage in a different kind of storytelling? One that embodies and facilitates healing and justice? Like Todd's, Sandercock's use of storytelling as methodology allows for a relational engagement with the field of her research, which centres on relationship, reciprocity, and approaching people and places with open ears rather than an open mouth. It also allows for an account of the ways in which her own personal transformations reflect back on her engagements with the community and her research. By interrogating her own positionality, laying bare her own privileges and transformations, she brings into clearer view the complexity and meaning of the interventions and observations she makes in her work.

Mitchell-Foster and de Leeuw, like Todd and Sandercock, approach storytelling as a means to shift from an inquiry of the mind to one of the heart. Rather than seek to push emotion and feeling to the side, they are inspired by Indigenous scholars to bring these tools to the forefront of their analysis by centring their research practice—their methodology—around story. Also invoking the relational nature of storytelling, Mitchell-Foster and de Leeuw argue that story provides a language through which people can truly understand each other, for it is a language to which everyone has access. Through ArtDays, stories produced and shared by a small northern rural First Nations community have enabled the experiential engagement of medical students and trainees with the strengths and challenges lived in that community. These narratives become a way for health care professionals to understand their own practices and the impacts of these practices on First Nations clients, relationally and across time and space. Perhaps most profoundly, storytelling provides a conduit through which the (largely) non-Indigenous population of medical students and trainees in the University of Northern British Columbia's health care programs can begin to know Indigenous peoples and places as well as critically reflect on themselves, their positionalities, historical and present-day injustices and inequalities in health care, and the need for culturally safe health care support and services. Importantly, Mitchell-Foster and de Leeuw found that storytelling through arts-based methodologies facilitated the creation of a safe space, where First Nations community members felt they could express themselves in a respectful, culturally safe environment and medical students and trainees felt they could engage with the difficult subjects of settler guilt and socially ingrained anti-Indigenous racism in a supportive environment. In this way, ArtDays has also brought the heart front and centre in medical students' training, which is critical to employing storytelling not as simply a method, or even a methodology, but as an epistemology.

While the development and application of storytelling as methodology is a key contribution in this book, and its potential for the reorientation of Indigenous and settler relations is explored, considerable challenges remain to the widespread acceptance of storytelling within the academy. Though creative and arts-based practices are encountered more frequently in academic research, they remain experimental in most disciplines. What's more, storytelling in the context of research with and by Indigenous peoples is not simply a method that can be slotted neatly into research proposals. More than a research tool, it is an entire approach towards research that is relational, reciprocal, and respectful. It is our hope that this book has opened up a deeper discussion around the various ways in which such an approach might be mobilized.

Storytelling to Take Back Space for Indigenous (and Other Culturally Embedded) Ways of Knowing

The knowledge of Indigenous people has always been here, and the persistent power of storytelling is testament to epistemologies that have not been extinguished despite the efforts of colonial powers and projects. Episkenew's (2009) recognition of the healing power of storytelling is an understanding that it is through taking back space (or, like the title of her book, "Tak[ing] Back Our Spirits") for Indigenous stories that healing takes place. This taking back of space, following Episkenew, enables Indigenous stories not only to empower Indigenous writers and readers but also to re-educate mainstream settler colonial audiences by promoting alternative stories to those that have dominated colonial pasts and presents. For both Todd and Kolson, using storytelling in their work is a way to take back and hold space for Indigenous epistemologies. In fact, Todd asserts that storytelling is a means to speak back to Empire by reasserting Indigenous presence within a Eurocentric and colonial academic tradition. The path that scholars like Todd work to clear is one that reveals the myriad culturally embedded knowledges that have been similarly undermined or even silenced. Kolson, meanwhile, offers a window into the experiences of life in northern Indigenous communities, so often characterized as remote outposts on a Canadian frontier. Through her story about a young woman's introduction to the world beyond her community, Kolson uses narrative to reveal much about the nuances and complexities of daily life, childhood, and change in a northern community. Kolson, like Todd, uses storytelling to delicately open up themes of Indigenous resilience.

Though contributors like Sandercock and Wong are not themselves Indigenous, they engage with storytelling to write relationally and reciprocally with Indigenous peoples and places. In this sense, their writing serves as an important witness to Indigenous knowledges by underlining the relevance, strength, and necessity of storytelling, both as a form of knowledge transmission and as a form of knowledge in itself. For Wong, "sleepless in Somba K'e" is a form of respect and reverence for the traditional homelands of the Yellowknives Dene, upon which she found herself a visitor. The act of storytelling allows for witnessing not only as a form of description or knowledge sharing but also as a mode of reciprocity, through the expression of one's gratitude, experiences, and love. Moore, Spencer, Leggatt, and Stewart also reassert Indigenous knowledges by studying Indigenous stories not as objects or ethnographies but, rather, as living, breathing innovations and representations. In Moore's chapter, Indigenous storytellers shift from their Indigenous languages to English and back again, a practice that, Moore argues, does not lessen the authenticity of the stories or their tellers but rather demonstrates a high linguistic sophistication—that enhances the stories rather than diminishing them. Moore's analysis challenges dominant ideologies by arguing that bilingual narratives are as representative of Indigenous knowledges and realities as stories in Indigenous languages alone. While scholars working with Indigenous languages may prefer the latter, he argues, this is the result of viewing Indigenous stories through an outside gaze; code-switching is an intellectual achievement, not a shortcoming. In making this argument, Moore effectively works to realign Eurocentric and conventional scholarly thought on Indigenous language and storytelling. Spencer, meanwhile, also avoids approaching Indigenous stories as objects to study through a purely western academic lens, instead gleaning a much deeper understanding through her efforts to view the stories of François Mandeville from his perspective as a Métis-Chipewyan trapper, always in movement and always the forerunner from one community to another. In Spencer's reading, hunting and trapping become, in effect, the generative spaces through which Indigenous epistemologies spring forth: a perpetual meeting place between Mandeville's physical and conceptual environments.

Stewart and Leggatt uncover historical and contemporary stories in the visual and audible urban landscape of Edmonton, Alberta, in order to attend to the significance of Indigeneity in the city. They do this by overturning the very tools through which they typically approach their surroundings:

not through sight alone, but through audible worlds made available to them through listening. Sound embodies relation and reciprocity, they suggest, because it necessarily implicates the listener, her body, her location, her state of being. Not only under the bridge but everywhere, the relations of Indigenous people to the city, and to the places upon which and from which it is built, are present. And yet the forms that these relations take are not, as Stewart and Leggatt find, determined by a Western European taxonomy. They can be seen and heard, therefore, only if the modes for recognizing them shift and open to include or (re)place Indigenous ways of knowing and understanding. Like those of Indigenous authors in this book, the contributions from non-Indigenous scholars contribute to the creation of meeting places between Indigenous epistemologies and the Eurocentric academy. Sandercock, Wong, Leggatt, and Stewart all use modes of storytelling as a way to both bear witness to the Indigenous peoples and places who have hosted them, and with whom they have entered into relationship, and also, in Sandercock's case, to dismantle the distancing structures inherent in conventional academic writing.

Collectively, the contributors to this collection take up Episkenew's call to challenge opaque or one-sided representations of Indigenous issues by underlining relationship and reciprocity. Attention to these two key elements is necessary as the authors navigate the murky pursuit of bringing different ways of knowing together in such a way that one (storytelling) does not become colonized by the other (the Eurocentric academic tradition). However, despite the spirit of relationship and reciprocity conveyed in this book, the ethical and just treatment and recognition of Indigenous stories in western academia is a goal that remains unattained. These stories and methodologies remain vulnerable to cooption or tokenism. Given the damage that has been inflicted on Indigenous epistemologies by colonial actors and policy-makers, the project of decolonization to which this book seeks to contribute remains large and open.

Storytelling and the Meaning of Activating the Heart

The core uniting theme of the Activating the Heart workshop and the resulting book is storytelling as a means to activate the heart through understanding, sharing, and creation. The original intent of the words "to activate the heart," as used by our friend and colleague Dawnis Kennedy, was to assert space for Indigenous and other culturally embedded ways of knowing by acknowledging and celebrating the power of the heart. Activating the heart through storytelling places emotion, relationships, reciprocity, recognition, and justice at the centre. In the context of Indigenous storytelling, activating the heart is not only a means through which the traumas of colonial policies and the resulting Indigenous–settler relationships can be addressed but, even more importantly, a place where paths towards community healing and renewal can be charted. When writing about Indigenous stories, however, we must always consider the capacity for these stories to be told detached from Indigenous epistemologies and practices—as a vast, destructive history has demonstrated. Contemporary forms of tokenism and colonization of Indigenous knowledges and lands are rampant. In response, the contributors here collectively assert that when the objective becomes to activate the heart through storytelling, creating intellectual and methodological space for different perspectives and positionalities to see and ultimately understand one another, the dynamism of storytelling as a tool to understand, share, and create is recognized. This approach resists storytelling as a formulaic method that can be slotted into a research proposal to satisfy cross-cultural research requirements, because it insists upon the building and maintenance of ever-evolving relationships—relationships that are critical to a meaningful and shared journey towards reconciliation. In this sense, the chapters in this book do not promote the (often tokenizing) *inclusion* of Indigenous methodologies within the academy but, rather, call for a fundamental rethinking and reorientation around what constitutes knowledge in the first place, and how we might cease to privilege certain modes of knowledge sharing over others. The call for such a fundamental rethinking is not new: in fact, it is one of the calls to action outlined by the Truth and Reconciliation Commission of Canada. The need for storytelling to understand, to share, and to create has never been greater, as the path towards substantive reconciliation in Canada remains an elusive one. Indigenous stories cannot simply serve as objects or symbols; rather, they must serve as a form for new relationships and for ethical and just recognition. In this sense, this book, with its exploration of storytelling as a means to reorient research methodologies and take back space for Indigenous knowledges within the academy, does not exist in a vacuum. Rather, it exists in reflexive dialogue with much larger debates around the meaning of reconciliation within a (post)colonial academy, how Indigenous and non-Indigenous scholars can engage in responsible, reciprocal relationships with the people and places with whom they work and engage, and how to advance a reorientation of the academy towards a multiplicity of culturally embedded knowledge forms and practices.

References

Agamben, Giorgio. 2002. *Remnants of Auschwitz: The Witness and the Archive.* New York: Zone.

———. 2004. *The Open: Man and Animal.* Stanford, CA: Stanford University Press.

Alfred, Taiaiake, and Jeff Corntassel. 2005. "Being Indigenous: Resurgences against Contemporary Colonialism." *Government and Opposition* 40 (4): 597–614. https://doi.org/10.1111/j.1477-7053.2005.00166.x.

Allard, Yvon E. 2007. *Métis Concepts of Health: Placing Health within Social Cultural Context—Social, Economic, and Environmental (Ecological) Determinants of Métis Health.* Ottawa: Métis National Council.

Archibald, Jo-ann. 2008. *Indigenous Storywork: Educating the Heart, Mind, Body and Spirit.* Vancouver: UBC Press.

Arntfield, Shannon L., Kristen Slesar, Jennifer Dickson, and Rita Charon. 2013. "Narrative Medicine as a Means of Training Medical Students Towards Residency Competences." *Patient Education and Counseling* 91 (3): 280–86. https://doi.org/10.1016/j.pec.2013.01.014. PMID:23462070.

Attili, Giovanni, and Leonie Sandercock. 2007. *Where Strangers Become Neighbours.* 50-minute documentary. Montreal: National Film Board of Canada.

———. 2010. *Finding Our Way.* 90-minute documentary. Vancouver: Moving Images.

Auer, Peter. 1995. "The Pragmatics of Code-Switching." In *One Speaker, Two Languages: Cross-Disciplinary Perspectives on Code-Switching,* edited by Lesley Milroy and Pieter Muysken, 115–35. Cambridge: Cambridge University Press. https://doi.org/10.1017/CBO9780511620867.006.

Baba, Lauren. 2013. *Cultural Safety in First Nations, Inuit and Métis Public Health: Environmental Scan of Cultural Competency and Safety in Education, Training and Health Services.* Prince George, BC: National Collaborating Centre for Aboriginal Health.

Ball, Jessica. 2008. "Cultural Safety in Practice with Children, Families and Communities." Poster presented at the Early Years Inter-professional Research and Practice Conference, Vancouver, 30 January–2 February.

Barry, Janice, and Libby Porter. 2012. "Indigenous Recognition in State-Based Planning Systems: Understanding Textual Mediation in the Contact Zone." *Planning Theory* 11 (2): 170–87. https://doi.org/10.1177/1473095 211427285.

Bates, Victoria, Alan Bleakley, and Sam Goodman, eds. 2014. *Medicine, Health and the Arts: Approaches to the Medical Humanities.* London: Routledge.

Battiste, Marie. 2014. "Ambidextrous Epistemologies: Indigenous Knowledge with the Indigenous Renaissance." In *Critical Collaborations: Indigeneity, Diaspora, and Ecology in Canadian Literary Studies,* edited by Smaro Kamboureli and Christl Verduyn, 83–98. Waterloo, ON: Wilfrid Laurier University Press.

Belfrage, Mary. 2007. "Why 'Culturally Safe' Health Care?" *Medical Journal of Australia* 186 (10): 537–38. PMID:17516905.

Bocking, Stephen. 2005. "The Nature of Cities: Perspectives in Canadian Urban Environmental History." *Urban History Review* 34 (1): 3–8. https:// doi.org/10.7202/1016043ar.

Bourassa, Carrie, Kim McKay-McNabb, and Mary Hampton. 2005. "Racism, Sexism and Colonialism: The Impact on the Health of Aboriginal Women in Canada." *Canadian Woman Studies* 24 (1): 23–30.

Bourke, Lisa, Collette Sheridan, Ursula Russell, Graeme Jones, Dawn DeWitt, and Siaw-Teng Liaw. 2004. "Developing a Conceptual Understanding of Rural Health Practice." *Australian Journal of Rural Health* 12 (5): 181–86. https://doi.org/10.1111/j.1440-1854.2004.00601.x. PMID:15588259.

Brennan, Timothy. 2001. "Angry Beauty and Literary Love: An *Orientalism* for All Time." In *Revising Culture, Reinventing Peace: The Influence of Edward W. Said,* edited by Naseer Hasan Aruri and Muhammad A. Shuraydi, 86–99. New York: Olive Branch Press.

Bringhurst, Robert. 2009. Foreword. In *This Is What They Say: A Story Cycle Dictated in Northern Alberta in 1928,* by François Mandeville, edited and translated by Ronald Scollon, 7–12. Vancouver: Douglas and McIntyre.

British Columbia Provincial Health Officer. 2009. *Pathways to Health and Healing—2nd Report on the Health and Wellbeing of Aboriginal People in British Columbia. Provincial Health Officer's Annual Report 2007.* Victoria: Ministry of Healthy Living and Sport.

Brodkin, Karen, Sandra Morgen, and Janis Hutchinson. 2011. "Anthropology as White Public Space?" *American Anthropologist* 113 (4): 545–56. https://doi.org/10.1111/j.1548-1433.2011.01368.x.

Brody, Hugh. [1981] 2004. *Maps and Dreams: Indians and the British Columbia Frontier.* Vancouver: Douglas and McIntyre.

Browne, Anette J., Victoria L. Smye, and Colleen Varcoe. 2005. "The Relevance of Postcolonial Theoretical Perspectives to Research in Aboriginal Health." *Canadian Journal of Nursing Research* 37 (4): 16–37. PMID:16541817.

Browne, Annette J., and Colleen Varcoe. 2006. "Critical Cultural Perspectives and Health Care Involving Aboriginal Peoples." *Contemporary Nurse* 22 (2): 155–67. https://doi.org/10.5172/conu.2006.22.2.155. PMID:17026422.

Bunch, Martin J., Karen E. Morrison, Margot W. Parkes, and Henry D. Venema. 2011. "Promoting Health and Well-Being by Managing for Social-Ecological Resilience: The Potential of Integrating EcoHealth and Water Resources Management Approaches." *Ecology and Society* 16 (1): article 6. https://doi.org/10.5751/ES-03803-160106.

Burnham, Clint, and Christine Stewart, eds. 2011. "21st-Century Poetics." Special issue, *Canadian Literature* 210/211.

Cameron, Anne. 1981. *Daughters of Copper Woman.* Vancouver: Press Gang Publishers.

Canada, Royal Commission on Aboriginal Peoples [RCAP]. 1996. *Report of the Royal Commission on Aboriginal Peoples.* Ottawa: Royal Commission on Aboriginal Peoples.

Canada Council for the Arts. 2010. *Expressions: Canadian Aboriginal Artists.* Ottawa: Canada Council for the Arts.

Canadian Institutes of Health Research [CIHR], Natural Sciences and Engineering Research Council of Canada [NSERC], and Social Sciences and Humanities Research Council of Canada [SSHRC]. 2010. *Tri-Council*

Policy Statement: Ethical Conduct for Research Involving Humans. Ottawa: Government of Canada.

Chandler, Michael J., and Christopher Lalonde. 1998. "Cultural Continuity as a Hedge against Suicide in Canada's First Nations." *Transcultural Psychiatry* 35 (2): 191–219. https://doi.org/10.1177/136346159803500202.

Chandler, Michael, Christopher Lalonde, Bryan W. Sokol, and Darcy Hallett, eds. 2003. *Personal Persistence, Identity Development, and Suicide: A Study of Native and Non-Native North American Adolescents.* With commentary by James E. Marcia. Boston: Blackwell.

Charon, Rita. 2001. "Narrative Medicine: A Model for Empathy, Reflection, Profession, and Trust." *Journal of the American Medical Association* 286 (15): 1897–902. https://doi.org/10.1001/jama.286.15.1897. PMID:11597295.

———. 2004. "Narrative and Medicine." *New England Journal of Medicine* 350 (9): 862–64. https://doi.org/10.1056/NEJMp038249. PMID:14985483.

———. 2006. "The Self-Telling Body." In "Narrative—State of the Art," edited by Michael Bamberg. Special issue, *Narrative Inquiry* 16 (1): 191–200.

Chastonay, Philippe, Véronique Zesiger, Axel Klohn, Ludivine Soguel, Emmanuel Kabengele Mpinga, Nu Viet Vu, and Laurent Berheim. 2013. "Development and Evaluation of a Community Immersion Program during Preclinical Medical Studies: A 15-Year Experience at the University of Geneva Medical School." *Advances in Medical Education and Practice* 4: 69–76.

Clifford, James. 1980. "Fieldwork, Reciprocity, and the Making of Ethnographic Texts: The Example of Maurice Leenhardt." *Man* (n.s.) 15 (3): 518–32. https://doi.org/10.2307/2801348.

———. 2004. "Looking Several Ways: Anthropology and Native Heritage in Alaska." *Current Anthropology* 45 (1): 5–30. https://doi.org/10.2307/2801348.

Cornwall, Andrea, and Rachel Jewkes. 1995. "What Is Participatory Research?" *Social Science and Medicine* 41 (12): 1667–676. https://doi.org/10.1016/0277-9536(95)00127-S. PMID:8746866.

Cox, Susan M., Darquise Lafrenière, Pamela Brett-MacLean, Kate Collie, Nancy Cooley, Janet Dunbrack, and Gerri Frager. 2010. "Tipping the Iceberg: The State of Arts and Health in Canada." *Arts and Health* 2 (2): 109–24. https://doi.org/10.1080/17533015.2010.481291.

Crampton, Peter, Anthony Dowell, Chris Parkin, and Caroline Thompson. 2003. "Combating Effects of Racism through a Cultural Immersion Medical Education Program." *Academic Medicine* 78 (6): 595–98. https://doi .org/10.1097/00001888-200306000-00008. PMID:12805038.

Creswell, John W. 2009. *Research Design: Qualitative, Quantitative and Mixed Methods Approaches.* Thousand Oaks, CA: Sage Publications.

Cruikshank, Julie. 1998. *The Social Life of Stories: Narrative and Knowledge in the Yukon Territory.* Vancouver: UBC Press.

Currie, Cheryl L., T. Cameron Wild, Donald P. Schopflocher, Lory Laing, and Paul Veugelers. 2013. "Illicit and Prescription Drug Problems among Urban Aboriginal Adults in Canada: The Role of Traditional Culture in Protection and Resilience." *Social Science and Medicine* 88: 1–9. https:// doi.org/10.1016/j.socscimed.2013.03.032. PMID:23702204.

Curtis, Edward S. 1928. "Tseqi Tsatsane Hehohl'ai, Woman Copper She-found." In *The North American Indian.* Vol. 18, *The Chipewyan. The Western Woods Cree. The Sarsi,* 127–28. Norwood, MA: Plimpton Press.

Dancygier, Barbara. 2011. *The Language of Stories: A Cognitive Approach.* Cambridge: Cambridge University Press. https://doi.org/10.1017/ CBO9780511794414.

De Beers Canada. 2015. "Snap Lake Mine." Accessed 14 March 2015. https:// www.debeersgroup.com/canada/en/operations/mining/snap-lake.html.

de Leeuw, Sarah. 2004. *Unmarked: Landscapes along Highway 16.* Edmonton, AB: NeWest Press.

——. 2014. "Telling Stories about Stories." *Canadian Family Physician* 60 (1): 65–67. PMID:24452566.

de Leeuw, Sarah, Sean Maurice, Travis Holyk, Margo Greenwood, and Warner Adam. 2012. "With Reserves: Colonial Geographies and First Nations Health." *Annals of the Association of American Geographers* 102 (5): 904–11. https://doi.org/10.1080/00045608.2012.674897.

de Leeuw, Sarah, Margot W. Parkes, and Deborah Thien. 2014. "Questioning Medicine's Discipline: The Arts of Emotions in Undergraduate Medical Education." *Emotion, Space and Society* 11: 43–51.

de Leeuw, Sarah, Margot W. Parkes, Vanessa Sloan Morgan, Julia Christensen, Nicole Lindsay, Kendra Mitchell-Foster, and Julia Russell Jozkow. 2017. "Going Unscripted: A Call to Critically Engage Storytelling Methods and

Methodologies in Geography and the Medical-Health Sciences." *The Canadian Geographer / Le Géographe canadien.* https://doi.org/10.1111/cag.12337.

Deleuze, Gilles, and Félix Guattari. [1980] 2007. "Becoming-Animal." From "1730: Becoming-Intense, Becoming-Animal, Becoming-Imperceptible …" Reprint, *The Animals Reader: The Essential Classic and Contemporary Writings,* edited by Linda Kalof and Amy Fitzgerald, 37–50. New York: Berg. [First published in English in *A Thousand Plateaus: Capitalism and Schizophrenia,* translated by Brian Massumi. Minneapolis: University of Minnesota Press, 1987.]

Deloria, Vine, Jr. 1999. "A Flock of Anthros." In *Spirit and Reason: The Vine Deloria Jr. Reader,* 123–26. Golden, CO: Fulcrum Publishing.

Derrida, Jacques. [1997] 2002. "The Animal That Therefore I Am (More to Follow)." 1997. Translated by David Wills. *Critical Inquiry* 28 (2): 369–418. https://doi.org/10.1086/449046.

Donald, Dwayne. 2012. "Indigenous Métissage: A Decolonizing Research Methodology." *International Journal of Qualitative Studies in Education* 25 (5): 533–55. https://doi.org/10.1080/09518398.2011.554449.

Donohoe, Martin T. 2010. "Stories and Society: Using Literature to Teach Medical Students about Public Health and Social Justice." *International Journal of Creative Arts in Interdisciplinary Practice* 8:1–21.

Dussault, Gilles, and Maria C. Franceschini. 2006. "Not Enough There, Too Many Here: Understanding Geographical Imbalances in the Distribution of the Health Workforce." *Human Resources for Health* 4 (1): 12. https://doi.org/10.1186/1478-4491-4-12. PMID:16729892.

Eng, Eugenia, Karen Strazza Moore, Scott D. Rhodes, Derek M. Griffith, Leo L. Allison, Kate Shirah, and Elvira M. Mebane. 2005. "Insiders and Outsiders Assess Who Is 'the Community': Participant Observation, Key Informant Interview, Focus Group Interview, and Community Forum." In *Methods in Community-Based Participatory Research for Health,* edited by Barbara A. Israel, Eugenia Eng, Amy J. Schulz, and Edith A. Parker, 77–100. San Francisco: Jossey-Bass.

Enns, Murray W., Brian J. Cox, Jitender Sareen, and Paul Freeman. 2001. "Adaptive and Maladaptive Perfectionism in Medical Students: A Longitudinal Investigation." *Medical Education* 35 (11): 1034–42. https://doi.org/10.1046/j.1365-2923.2001.01044.x. PMID:11703639.

Episkenew, Jo-Ann. 2009. *Taking Back Our Spirits: Indigenous Literature, Public Policy, and Healing.* Winnipeg: University of Manitoba Press.

Erfan, Aftab. 2013. "An Experiment in Therapeutic Planning: Learning with the Gwa'sala-'Nakwaxda'xw First Nations." PhD diss., University of British Columbia.

Erfan, Aftab, and Leonie Sandercock. 2012. "Plato's Lacunae: On the Value of Loving Attachment in Community-Based Planning Research and Practice." *Planning Theory and Practice* 13 (4): 620–27.

Evans, Mike, Chris Andersen, Devin Dietrich, Carrie Bourassa, Tricia Logan, Lawrence D. Berg, and Elizabeth Devolder. 2012. "Funding and Ethics in Métis Community Based Research: The Complications of a Contemporary Context." *International Journal of Critical Indigenous Studies* 5 (1): 54–66.

Feld, Steven. 1996. "Waterfalls of Song: An Acoustemology of Place Resounding in Bosavi, Papua New Guinea." In *Senses of Place,* edited by Steven Feld and Keith H. Basso, 91–136. Santa Fe, CA: School of American Research.

Ferrara, Nadia. 2004. *Healing through Art: Ritualized Space and Cree Identity.* Montreal and Kingston: McGill-Queen's University Press.

Fiske, Edward B., ed. 1999. *Champions of Change: The Impact of the Arts on Learning.* Washington, DC: President's Committee on the Arts and Humanities.

Forget, Gilles. 2001. "Better Ecosystem Management for Improved Human Health: The Ecosystem Approach to Human Health." In *Challenges and Strategies for Implementing the Ecosystem Approach to Human Health in Developing Countries: Reflections from Regional Consultations,* edited by Gabriella Feola and Roberto Bazzani, 56–58. Montevideo: International Development Research Centre, Regional Office for Latin America and the Caribbean. http://hdl.handle.net/10625/31156.

Forget, Gilles, and Jean Lebel. 2001. "An Ecosystem Approach to Human Health." *International Journal of Occupational and Environmental Health* 7 (2 Supplement): S3–S38. PMID:11387989.

Franklin, John. 1823. *Narrative of a Journey to the Shores of the Polar Sea in the Years 1819, 20, 21, and 22: With an Appendix on Various Subjects Relating to Science and Natural History.* London: John Murray. https://doi.org/10.5479/sil.75582.39088002032894.

Friedmann, John. 1973. *Retracking America.* New York: Doubleday Anchor.

———. 1987. *Planning in the Public Domain: From Knowledge to Action.* Princeton, NJ: Princeton University Press.

Foucault, Michel. [1966] 1970. *The Order of Things: An Archaeology of the Human Sciences,* translated anonymously. London: Routledge.

Goddard, Pliny Earle. 1912. *Chipewyan Texts.* Vol. 10. Cambridge, MA: Harvard University Trustees.

Goulet, Jean-Guy A. 1998. *Ways of Knowing: Experience, Knowledge, and Power among the Dene Tha.* Vancouver: UBC Press.

Graveline, Fyre Jean. 2000. "Circle as Methodology: Enacting an Aboriginal Paradigm." *International Journal of Qualitative Studies in Education* 13 (4): 361–70. https://doi.org/10.5479/sil.75582.39088002032894.

Greenhalgh, Trisha, and Brian Hurwitz. 1999. "Narrative Based Medicine: Why Study Narrative?" *British Medical Journal* 318 (7175): 48–50. https://doi.org/10.1136/bmj.318.7175.48. PMID:9872892.

Gumperz, John. 1982. *Discourse Strategies.* Cambridge: Cambridge University Press. https://doi.org/10.1017/CBO9780511611834.

Gupta, Setu, Abhinav Agrawal, Satendra Singh, and Navjeevan Singh. 2013. "Theatre of the Oppressed in Medical Humanities Education: The Road Less Travelled." *Indian Journal of Medical Ethics* 10 (3): 200–203. PMID:23912737.

Hall, Edward. 2013. "Making and Gifting Belonging: Creative Arts and People with Learning Disabilities." *Environment & Planning A* 45 (2): 244–62. https://doi.org/10.1068/a44629.

Halperin, Edward C. 2010. "Preserving the Humanities in Medical Education." *Medical Teacher* 32 (1): 76–79. https://doi.org/10.3109/014215909 03390585. PMID:20095779.

Healey, Patsy. 2007. *Collaborative Planning.* 2nd ed. London: Macmillan.

Hearne, Samuel. 1795. *A Journey from Prince of Wales' Fort in Hudson's Bay to the Northern Ocean in the Years 1769, 1770, 1771, and 1772.* London: Strahan and Cadell.

Heavy Head, Ryan. 2005. "Feeding Sublimity: Embodiment in Blackfoot Experience." MA thesis, University of Lethbridge, AB.

Helm, June, with Teresa S. Carterette and Nancy O. Lurie. 2000. *The People of Denendeh: Ethnohistory of the Indians of Canada's Northwest Territories.* Iowa City: University of Iowa Press.

Henry, Barbara R., Shane Houston, and Gavin H. Mooney. 2004. "Institutional Racism in Australian Healthcare: A Plea for Decency." *Medical Journal of Australia* 180 (10): 517–20. PMID:15139829.

hooks, bell. 2000. *All about Love: New Visions.* New York: Harper Collins.

Hunt, Sarah. 2014. "Ontologies of Indigeneity: The Politics of Embodying a Concept." *Cultural Geographies* 21 (1): 27–32. https://doi.org/10.1177/1474474013500226.

Hurwitz, Brian. 2000. "Narrative and the Practice of Medicine." *The Lancet* 356 (9247): 2086–89. https://doi.org/10.1016/S0140-6736(00)03412-7. PMID:11145506.

Hymes, Dell. 2003. "Use All There Is to Use." In *Now I Know Only So Far: Essays in Ethnopoetics,* 36–80. Lincoln: University of Nebraska Press.

The Invisible Committee. 2009. *The Coming Insurrection.* Cambridge, MA: MIT Press.

Irlbacher-Fox, Stephanie. 2009. *Finding Dahshaa. Self-Government, Social Suffering, and Aboriginal Policy in Canada.* Vancouver: UBC Press.

Israel, Barbara A., Eugenia Eng, Amy J. Schulz, and Edith A. Parker. 2005. "Introduction to Methods in Community-Based Participatory Research for Health." In *Methods in Community-Based Participatory Research for Health,* edited by Barbara A. Israel, Eugenia Eng, Amy J. Schulz, and Edith A. Parker, 3–26. San Francisco: Jossey-Bass.

Jackson, Michael. [2002] 2006. *The Politics of Storytelling: Violence, Transgression, and Intersubjectivity.* Copenhagen: Museum Tusculanum Press.

Jacobson, Roman. 1966. "On Linguistic Aspects of Translation." In *On Translation,* edited by Reuben A. Brower, 232–39. New York: Oxford University Press.

Jameson, Frederic. 2009. *Valences of the Dialectic.* London: Verso.

Jensen, Tina. 2013. "Elk Herd Found Dead in Northeastern N.M." *KRQE News.* Accessed 20 November 2014. https://web.archive.org/web/20131226140853.

Johnson, R. Burke, and Anthony J. Onwuegbuzie. 2004. "Mixed Methods Research: A Research Paradigm Whose Time Has Come." *Educational Researcher* 33 (7): 14–26. https://doi.org/10.3102/0013189X033007014.

Johnson, R. Burke, Anthony J. Onwuegbuzie, and Lisa A. Turner. 2007. "Toward a Definition of Mixed Methods Research." *Journal of Mixed Methods Research* 1 (2): 112–33. https://doi.org/10.1177/1558689806298224.

Johnstone, P. Lynne. 2004. "Mixed Methods, Mixed Methodology Health Services Research in Practice." *Qualitative Health Research* 14 (2): 259–71. https://doi.org/10.1177/1049732303260610. PMID:14768461.

Jojola, Ted. 2008. "Indigenous Planning: An Emerging Paradigm." *Canadian Journal of Urban Research* 17 (1 Supplement): 37–47.

Kagawa-Singer, Marjorie, and Shaheen Kassim-Lakha. 2003. "A Strategy to Reduce Cross-Cultural Miscommunication and Increase the Likelihood of Improving Health Outcomes." *Academic Medicine* 78 (6): 577–87. https://doi.org/10.1097/00001888-200306000-00006. PMID:12805036.

Kahn, Douglas. 1999. *Noise Water Meat.* Cambridge, MA: MIT Press.

Kaska Tribal Council. 1999. *Kaska Gudeji: Kaska Narratives,* edited by Patrick Moore. Whitehorse, YT: Kaska Tribal Council.

Kelm, Mary-Ellen. 1998. *Colonizing Bodies: Aboriginal Health and Healing in British Columbia, 1900–50.* Vancouver: UBC Press.

Kiitokiiaapii. 2010. "Kiitokiiaapii Tells the Elk Woman Story." *Blackfoot Digital Library.* Accessed 20 November 2014. https://www.blackfoot digitallibrary.com/publication/kiitokiiaapii-tells-elk-woman-story.

King, Thomas. 2003. *The Truth about Stories: A Native Narrative.* Toronto: House of Anansi Press.

Klopp, Annika, and Allison Nakanishi. 2012. "Art Days: Two Medical Students Reflect on the Value of Cultural Immersion and Cultural Safety." *British Columbia Medical Journal* 54 (3): 126–29.

Kovach, Margaret. 2009. *Indigenous Methodologies: Characteristics, Conversations, Contexts.* Toronto: University of Toronto Press.

Kulick, Don. 1992. *Language Shift and Cultural Reproduction: Socialization, Self and Syncretism in a Papuan New Guinean Village.* New York: Cambridge University Press.

Kumagai, Arno K., and Delese Wear. 2014. "'Making Strange': A Role for the Humanities in Medical Education." *Academic Medicine* 89 (7): 973–77. https://doi.org/10.1097/ACM.0000000000000269. PMID:24751976.

LaBelle, Brandon. 2006. *Background Noise: Perspectives on Sound Art.* New York: Continuum.

———. 2010a. *Acoustic Territories: Sound Culture and Everyday Life.* New York: Continuum.

———. 2010b. "Sound as Hinge." In *Esemplasticism: The Truth Is a Compromise* [exhibition catalogue]. Berlin: TAG/Club Transmediale.

Lazzarino, Dave. 2013. "Official Names for Edmonton LRT Stops Unveiled." *Edmonton Sun*, 13 November. http://www.edmontonsun.com/2013/11/13/official-names-for-edmonton-lrt-stops-unveiled.

Lebel, Jean. 2003. *Health: An Ecosystem Approach*. Ottawa: International Development Research Centre.

Littlebear, Leroy. 2009. "Jagged Worldviews Colliding." In *Reclaiming Indignous Voice and Vision*, edited by Marie Battiste, 77–85. Vancouver: UBC Press.

Lukes, Steven. [1974] 2005. *Power: A Radical View*. 2nd ed. New York: Palgrave Macmillan. https://doi.org/10.1007/978-0-230-80257-5.

Mackrael, Kim. 2011. "UN Official Blasts 'Dire' Conditions in Attawapiskat." *Globe and Mail*, 20 December. Accessed 26 November 2013. http://www.theglobeandmail.com/news/politics/un-official-blasts-dire-conditions-in-attawapiskat/article4085452/.

MacSwan, Jeff. 2005. "Codeswitching and Generative Grammar: A Critique of the MLF Model and Some Remarks on 'Modified Minimalism.'" *Bilingualism: Language and Cognition* 8 (1): 1–22. https://doi.org/10.1017/S1366728904002068.

Mandeville, François. 1976. *Chipewyan Texts*. Translated by Fang Kuei Li and Ronald Scollon. Taipei: Academia Sinica.

———. 2009. *This Is What They Say: A Story Cycle Dictated in Northern Alberta in 1928*, edited and translated by Ron Scollon. Vancouver: Douglas and McIntyre.

Marris, Peter. 1975. *Loss and Change*. London: Routledge and Kegan Paul.

Marrone, Sonia. 2007. "Understanding Barriers to Health Care: A Review of Disparities in Health Care Services among Indigenous Populations." *International Journal of Circumpolar Health* 66 (3): 188–98. https://doi.org/10.3402/ijch.v66i3.18254. PMID:17655060.

McAdam (Saysewahum), Sylvia. 2015. *Nationhood Interrupted: Revitalizing nêhiyaw Legal Systems*. Saskatoon, SK: Purich Publishing.

McIvor, Onowa, Art Napoleon, and Kerissa M. Dickie. 2009. "Language and Culture as Protective Factors for At-Risk Communities." *Journal of Aboriginal Health* 5 (1): 6–25.

McNiff, Shaun. 2008. "Arts-Based Research." In *Handbook of the Arts in Qualitative Research*, edited by J. Gary Knowles and Ardra L. Cole, 29–40. Thousand Oaks, CA: Sage Publications. https://doi.org/10.4135/9781452226545.n3.

Medicine, Beatrice, and Sue-Ellen Jacobs. 2001. *Learning to Be an Anthropologist and Remaining Native.* Urbana: University of Illinois Press.

Merleau-Ponty, Maurice. [ca. 1960] 1968. *The Visible and the Invisible: Followed by Working Notes,* edited by Claude Lefort, translated by Alphonso Lingis. Evanston, IL: Northwestern University Press.

Mertens, Donna M. 2003. "Mixed Methods and the Politics of Human Research: The Transformative-Emancipatory Perspective." In *Handbook of Mixed Methods in Social and Behavioral Research,* edited by Abbas Tashakkori and Charles Teddlie, 135–64. Thousand Oaks, CA: Sage Publications.

Minkler, Meredith. 2000. "Using Participatory Action Research to Build Healthy Communities." *Public Health Reports* 115 (2–3): 191–97. https://doi.org/10.1093/phr/115.2.191. PMID:10968753.

———. 2004. "Ethical Challenges for the 'Outside' Researcher in Community-Based Participatory Research." *Health Education and Behavior* 31 (6): 684–97.

———. 2005. "Community-Based Research Partnerships: Challenges and Opportunities." *Journal of Urban Health* 82 (2 Supplement 2): ii3–ii12. PMID:15888635.

Minkler, Meredith, and Nina Wallerstein. 2003. "Introduction to Community Based Participatory Research." In *Community-Based Participatory Research for Health: From Process to Outcomes,* 2nd ed., edited by Meredith Minkler and Nina Wallerstein, 3–26. San Francisco: Jossey-Bass.

Monto, Tom. 2013. "Historic Tour of Mill Creek Ravine." *Old Alberta* Blog, 19 March. Accessed 26 November 2014. http://oldalberta.blogspot.ca/2013/03/historic-tour-of-mill-creek-ravine.html.

Moore, Patrick. 2007. "Negotiated Identities: The Evolution of Dene Tha and Kaska Personal Naming Systems." *Anthropological Linguistics* 49 (3–4): 283–307.

Moure, Erín. 2009. "The Anti-Anæsthetic." In *My Beloved Wager: Essays from a Writing Practice,* edited by Smaro Kamboureli, 21–34. Edmonton, AB: NeWest.

Muirhead, Alice, and Sarah de Leeuw. 2012. "Art and Wellness: The Importance of Art for Aboriginal Peoples' Health and Healing." In *Emerging Priorities,* edited by the National Collaborating Centre for Aboriginal Health, 1–8. Prince George, BC: National Collaborating Centre for Aboriginal Health.

Murray, Richard B., Sarah Larkins, Heather Russell, Shaun Ewen, and David Prideaux. 2012. "Medical Schools as Agents of Change: Socially Accountable Medical Education." *Medical Journal of Australia* 196 (10): article 653. https://doi.org/10.5694/mja11.11473. PMID:22676883.

Myers-Scotton, Carol. 1997. *Duelling Languages: Grammatical Structure in Code-Switching.* Oxford: Oxford University Press.

———. 2004. "Precision Tuning of the Matrix Language Frame (MLF) Model of Code-Switching." *Sociolinguistica* 18: 106–17.

Nagy, Murielle. 2012. "Access to Data and Reports after Completion of a Project." *Études inuit. Inuit Studies* 35 (1–2): 201–21.

National Aboriginal Health Organization. 2010. *Principles of Ethical Métis Research.* Accessed 12 December 2012. http://www.naho.ca/documents/metis centre/english/PrinciplesofEthicalMetisResearch-descriptive_001.pdf.

Nguyen, Hung The. 2008. "Patient Centred Care: Cultural Safety in Indigenous Health." *Australian Family Physician* 37 (12): 990–94.

Nussbaum, Martha. 2001. *Upheavals of Thought: The Intelligence of Emotions.* Cambridge: Cambridge University Press. https://doi.org/10.1017/CBO 9780511840715.

Oliveros, Pauline. 2005. *Deep Listening: A Composer's Sound Practice.* Lincoln, NE: iUniverse.

Panther, Klaus-Uwe. 2006. "Metonymy as a Usage Event." *Cognitive Linguistics: Current Applications and Future Perspectives,* edited by Gitte Kristiansen, Michel Achard, Rene Dirven, and Francisco Ruiz de Mendoza Ibañez, 147–86. New York: Mouton de Gruyter.

Papps, Elaine, and Irihapeti Ramsden. 1996. "Cultural Safety in Nursing: The New Zealand Experience." *International Journal for Quality in Health Care* 8 (5): 491–97. https://doi.org/10.1093/intqhc/8.5.491. PMID:9117203.

Parkes, Margot W., Jerry Spiegel, Jaime Breilh, Fabio Cabarcas, Robert Huish, and Annalee Yassi. 2009. "Promoting the Health of Marginalized Populations in Ecuador through International Collaboration and Educational Innovations." *Bulletin of the World Health Organization* 87 (4): 312–19. https://doi.org/10.2471/BLT.07.045393. PMID:19551240.

Pelias, Ron. 2004. *A Methodology of the Heart.* New York: Altamira Press.

Petitot, Émile. [1886] 2010. *Traditions indiennes du Canada nord-ouest.* Paris: Maisonneuve et C. Leclerc. Reprint, Early Canadiana Online. http://eco .canadiana.ca/view/oocihm.15869.

Polaschek, N. R. 1998. "Cultural Safety: A New Concept in Nursing People of Different Ethnicities." *Journal of Advanced Nursing* 27 (3): 452–57. https://doi.org/10.1046/j.1365-2648.1998.00547.x. PMID:9543029.

Porter, Libby. 2010. *Unlearning the Colonial Cultures of Planning.* London: Ashgate.

Pratt, Mary Louise. 1992. *Imperial Eyes: Travel Writing and Transculturation.* London: Routledge. https://doi.org/10.4324/9780203163672.

Rancière, Jacques. [1987] 1991. "An Intellectual Adventure." In *The Ignorant Schoolmaster: Five Lessons in Intellectual Emancipation,* translated by Kristin Ross, 1–18. Stanford, CA: Stanford University Press.

Raw, Anni, Sue Lewis, Andrew Russell, and Jane Macnaughton. 2012. "A Hole in the Heart: Confronting the Drive for Evidence-Based Impact Research in Arts and Health." *Arts & Health* 4 (2): 97–108. https://doi.org/10.1080/17533015.2011.619991. PMID:24244217.

Regan, Paulette. 2011. *Unsettling the Settler Within.* Vancouver: UBC Press.

Richmond, Chantelle A. M., and Nancy A. Ross. 2009. "The Determinants of First Nation and Inuit Health: A Critical Population Health Approach." *Health and Place* 15 (2): 403–11. https://doi.org/10.1016/j.healthplace.2008.07.004. PMID:18760954.

Ridington, Robin. 1978. *Swan People: A Study of the Dunne-za Prophet Dance.* Ottawa: National Museums of Canada.

———. 1990. *Little Bit Know Something: Stories in a Language of Anthropology.* Iowa City: University of Iowa Press.

Ridington, Robin, and Jillian Ridington. 2006. *When You Sing It Now, Just Like New: First Nations Poetics, Voices, and Representations.* Lincoln: University of Nebraska Press.

Sandercock, Leonie. 2003. *Cosmopolis 2: Mongrel Cities of the 21st Century.* London: Continuum.

Sandercock, Leonie, and Giovanni Attili. 2012. "Unsettling a Settler Society: Film, Phronesis and Collaborative Planning in Small Town Canada." In *Real Social Science,* edited by Bent Flyvbjerg, Todd Landman, and Sanford Schram, 137–66. Cambridge: Cambridge University Press. https://doi.org/10.1017/CBO9780511719912.010.

———. 2013. "The Past as Present: Film as a Community Planning Intervention in Native/Non-Native Relations in British Columbia, Canada." In *Re-*

claiming Indigenous Planning, edited by Ryan Walker, Ted Jojola, and David Natcher, 60–93. Montreal and Kingston: McGill-Queen's University Press.

———. 2014. "Changing the Lens: Film as Action Research and Therapeutic Planning Practice." *Journal of Planning Education and Research* 34 (1): 19–29. https://doi.org/10.1177/0739456X13516499.

Scollon, Ronald. 2009. "The Narrative Ethnography of François Mandeville." In *This Is What They Say: A Story Cycle Dictated in Northern Alberta in 1928,* by François Mandeville, edited and translated by Ronald Scollon, 227–62. Vancouver: Douglas and McIntyre.

Scollon, Ronald, and Suzanne B. K. Scollon. 1979. *Linguistic Convergence: An Ethnography of Speaking at Fort Chipewyan, Alberta.* New York: Academic Press.

Shahid, Shaouli, Lizzie D. Finn, and Sandra C. Thompson. 2009. "Barriers to Participation of Aboriginal People in Cancer Care: Communication in the Hospital Setting." *Medical Journal of Australia* 190 (10): 574–79. PMID:19450207.

Shapiro, Johanna, Jack Coulehan, Delese Wear, and Martha Montello. 2009. "Medical Humanities and Their Discontents: Definitions, Critiques and Implications." *Medical Humanities* 84 (2): 192–98. PMID:19174663.

Silko, Leslie Marmon. 1977. *Ceremony.* New York: Viking.

———. 1998. "Interior and Exterior Landscapes: The Pueblo Migration Stories." In *Speaking for the Generations: Native Writers on Writing,* edited by Simon J. Ortiz, 3–24. Tucson: University of Arizona Press.

Simpson, Audra. 2007. "On Ethnographic Refusal: Indigeneity, 'Voice' and Colonial Citizenship." *Junctures* 9: 67–80.

———. 2014. *Mohawk Interruptus: Political Life across the Borders of Settler States.* Durham, NC: Duke University Press.

Smith, Linda Tuhiwai. 1999. *Decolonizing Methodologies.* London: Zed Books.

———. 2012. *Decolonizing Methodologies,* 2nd ed. London: Zed Books.

Smye, Vicki, and Annette J. Browne. 2002. "'Cultural Safety' and the Analysis of Health Policy Affecting Aboriginal People." *Nurse Researcher* 9 (3): 42–56. https://doi.org/10.7748/nr2002.04.9.3.42.c6188. PMID:11985147.

South Slave Divisional Education Council. 2012. *Dëne Dédliné Yatié Perehtł'íscho Denínu Kuę́ Yatié, Chipewyan Dictionary.* Fort Smith, NT: South Slave Divisional Education Council.

Spenser, Edmund. 1909. *The Faerie Queene*, edited by J. C. Smith. 2 vols. Oxford: Clarendon.

Stanger-Ross, Jordan. 2008. "Municipal Colonialism in Vancouver: City Planning and the Conflict Over Indian Reserves." *Canadian Historical Review* 89 (4): 541–80. https://doi.org/10.3138/chr.89.4.541.

Stewart, Christine. 2015. "Propositions from under Mill Creek Bridge: A Practice of Reading." In *Sustaining the West: Cultural Responses, Past and Present,* edited by Lisa Piper and Lisa Szabo, 241–58. Waterloo, ON: Wilfrid Laurier University Press.

Stewart, Suzanne, Ted Riecken, Tish Scott, Michele Tanaka, and Janet Riecken. 2008. "Expanding Health Literacy: Indigenous Youth Creating Videos." *Journal of Health Psychology* 13 (2): 180–89. https://doi.org/ 10.1177/1359105307086709. PMID:18375624.

Stringer, Ernest T. 2007. *Action Research.* 3rd ed. Thousand Oaks, CA: Sage Publications.

Tang, Sannie Y., and Annette J. Browne. 2008. "'Race' Matters: Racialization and Egalitarian Discourses Involving Aboriginal People in the Canadian Health Care Context." *Ethnicity and Health* 13 (2): 109–27. https://doi .org/10.1080/13557850701830307. PMID:18425710.

Tashakkori, Abbas, and Charles Teddlie. 1998. *Mixed Methodology: Combining Qualitative and Quantitative Approaches.* Thousand Oaks, CA: Sage Publications.

———. 2003. "Major Issues and Controversies in the Use of Mixed Methods in the Social and Behavioural Sciences." In *Handbook of Mixed Methods in Social and Behavioral Research,* edited by Abbas Tashakkori and Charles Teddlie, 3–50. Thousand Oaks, CA: Sage Publications.

Teit, James. 1917. "Kaska Tales." *Journal of American Folklore* 30 (118): 427–73. https://doi.org/10.2307/534495.

Uexküll, Jakob von. 2010. *A Foray into the Worlds of Animals and Humans,* translated by Joseph D. O'Neil. Minneapolis: University of Minnesota Press.

Ulin, Priscilla R., Elizabeth T. Robinson, and Elizabeth E. Tolley. 2005. *Qualitative Methods in Public Health: A Field Guide for Applied Research.* San Francisco: Jossey-Bass.

Urrutia, Anselmo, and Joel Sherzer. 2000. "'The Way of the Cocoa Counsel' from the Kuna Indians of Panama." In *Translating Native Latin American Verbal Art: Ethnopoetics and Ethnography of Speaking,* edited by Kay

Sammons and Joel Sherzer, 141–57. Washington, DC: Smithsonian Institution Press.

Vaccarella, Maria. 2011. "Narrative Epileptology." *The Lancet* 377 (9764): 460–61. https://doi.org/10.1016/S0140-6736(11)60150-5. PMID:21300595.

Venne, Sharon. 1997. "Understanding Treaty 6: An Indigenous Perspective." In *Aboriginal Treaty Rights in Canada: Essays on Law, Equality, and Respect for Difference,* edited by Michael Asch, 173–207. Vancouver: UBC Press.

Voegelin, Salomé. 2010. *Listening to Noise and Silence: Towards a Philosophy of Sound Art.* New York: Continuum.

Walker, Roger, Helen Cromarty, Len Kelly, and Natalie St. Pierre-Hansen. 2009. "Achieving Cultural Safety in Aboriginal Health Services: Implementation of a Crosscultural Safety Model in a Hospital Setting." *Diversity in Health and Care* 6 (1): 11–22.

Wallerstein, Nina, and Bonnie Duran. 2003. "The Conceptual, Historical and Practice Roots of Community Based Participatory Research and Related Participatory Traditions." In *Community-Based Participatory Research for Health: From Process to Outcomes,* 2nd ed., edited by Meredith Minkler and Nina Wallerstein, 27–52. San Francisco: Jossey-Bass.

———. 2006. "Using Community-Based Participatory Research to Address Health Disparities." *Health Promotion Practice* 7 (3): 312–23. https://doi.org/10.1177/1524839906289376. PMID:16760238.

Wear, Delese. 2003. "Insurgent Multiculturalism: Rethinking How and Why We Teach Culture in Medical Education." *Academic Medicine* 78 (6): 549–54. https://doi.org/10.1097/00001888-200306000-00002. PMID:12805032.

Westerkamp, Hildegard. 2013. "Hildegard Westerkamp." Accessed 24 November 2014. http://mypage.siu.edu/honnav/project2/westerkamp.html.

Wiens, Jeanette. 2014. "Code-Switching and Language Ideology in a Northern Dene Community." MA thesis, University of Regina, SK.

Williams, Robyn. 1999. "Cultural Safety—What Does It Mean for Our Work Practice?" *Australian and New Zealand Journal of Public Health* 23 (2): 213–14. https://doi.org/10.1111/j.1467-842X.1999.tb01240.x. PMID:10330743.

Willson, Suzy. 2006. "What Can the Arts Bring to Medical Training?" *The Lancet* 368 (special issue): S15–16. https://doi.org/10.1016/S0140-6736 (06)69909-1.

Wilson, Shawn. 2008. *Research Is Ceremony.* Halifax, NS: Fernwood Publishing.

Žižek, Slavoj. 2000. *The Fragile Absolute: Or, Why Is the Christian Legacy Worth Fighting For?* London: Verso.

Zurba, Melanie, and Fikret Berkes. 2014. "Caring for Country through Participatory Art: Creating a Boundary Object for Communicating Indigenous Knowledge and Values." *Local Environment: The International Journal of Justice and Sustainability* 19 (8): 821–36. https://doi.org/10.1080/13549839.2013.792051.

About the Contributors

JULIA CHRISTENSEN is a geographer and writer, and lives and works on the ancestral and unceded homelands of the Mi'kmaq and Beothuk in St. John's, Newfoundland. She is a Tier II Canada Research Chair in Northern Governance and Public Policy at Memorial University (MUN), and her work focuses primarily on social, cultural, and health dimensions of housing and home in northern regions, with a particular emphasis on opportunities for Indigenizing northern social policy. As part and parcel of her research and community engagement, Julia works with various forms of research storytelling through her Research Storytelling Lab at MUN. She is the author of *No Home in a Homeland* (2017) and co-editor of *Indigenous Homelessness* (2016).

CHRISTOPHER COX is an Assistant Professor of Indigenous and minority-language issues in the School of Linguistics and Language Studies at Carleton University. His research centres on issues in language documentation, description, and revitalization, with a focus on the creation and application of permanent, accessible collections of language resources (*corpora*). For twenty years he has been involved with community-based language documentation, education, and revitalization efforts, most extensively in partnership with speakers of Plautdietsch, the traditional language of the Dutch-Russian Mennonites, and with Dene communities in Alberta and Yukon.

SARAH DE LEEUW is an Associate Professor with UNBC's Northern Medical Program, UBC's Faculty of Medicine, where she teaches and conducts research on the humanities and health inequities.

BREN KOLSON, who passed away while this volume was in production, was a Metis author, poet, and photographer born in Yellowknife, Northwest Territories, Canada, of Tso'Tine and Polish descent. Several of Ms. Kolson's poems were published in the anthology *Writing the Circle: Native Women of Western Canada* (1990). In 2005–6 Bren was shortlisted in the short-story category for the CBC Literary Awards. She attended the first Aboriginal Emerging Writers Residency at Banff, Alberta, and, in 2007, the Mother's Journey Writers Retreat at the Quesnel River in British Columbia with renowned author Maria Campbell and ten Indigenous Canadian writers. Bren's book *Myth of the Barrens* was published in 2009. In 2017 Ms. Kolson's book about the barrenlands was chosen by the Book Excellence Award Team in the finalists category. Her short story "You Must Have Been a Beautiful Lady" was published in 2017 as well as a second short story, "Old Rawhide Died." Bren wrote novels, short stories, essays, poetry, and prose. She lived in Yellowknife with her artistically talented daughter Kiera-Dawn Kolson.

Vancouver composer JACQUELINE LEGGATT has written music for theatre, dance, and concert performance. Although known for her chamber music, electroacoustics has become an essential part of her oeuvre, especially through collaborative works with language poets Catriona Strang, Nancy Shaw, and Christine Stewart. Leggatt's music has been performed in New York, Paris, Hong Kong, San Diego, Italy, and throughout Canada. She is a founding member of the Institute for Domestic Research and currently teaches at the Vancouver Academy of Music.

KENDRA MITCHELL-FOSTER lives and works in Prince George, BC. She is currently undertaking a master's in Theological Studies, continues to author work on social justice and heath equity, and is focused on community building projects in northern British Columbia.

PATRICK MOORE is Associate Professor of Anthropology at the University of British Columbia. He has worked with Dene (Athabaskan) languages, including Kaska, Dene Dháh (Slavey) and Dene-ẕaa Záágéʔ (Beaver) for over four decades. He has contributed to several works, including *Wolverine: Myths and Visions* and *Dene Gedeni: Traditional Lifestyles of Kaska Women, Dene Gudeji: Kaska Narratives Gūzāgi K'úgé'*, a Kaska, Mountain Slavey and Sekani noun dictionary, and the Virtual Museum of Canada *Dane Wajich* exhibit.

LEONIE SANDERCOCK co-chairs the Indigenous Community Planning program in the School of Community & Regional Planning at UBC. Her main interest is in working with First Nations, through collaborative community planning, using the medium of film as a catalyst for dialogue, healing, community development, and cultural revitalization. Her current project is a community-driven feature film (*Edge of the Knife*) in partnership with the Haida Nation and the Inuit film production company Kingulliit. Books include *Making the Invisible Visible* (1998), *Towards Cosmopolis: Planning for Multicultural Cities* (1998), *Cosmopolis 2: Mongrel Cities of the 21st Century* (2003), and *Multimedia Explorations in Urban Policy & Planning* (2010). Documentaries include *Where Strangers Become Neighbours* (2007) and *Finding Our Way (beyond Canada's apartheid)* (2010).

JASMINE SPENCER studies Dene/Athabaskan languages and literatures, with a research focus on animal stories. At present, she is a SSHRC postdoctoral research fellow at the University of Victoria, working with Leslie Saxon as well as Keren Rice, and a postdoctoral visiting research fellow at the Rothermere American Institute at Oxford University. Research projects include a recently completed dissertation titled "Telling Animals: A Histology of Dene Orature," a current postdoctoral research project titled "'Animal grammar': Documentation of poetics in northern and southern Dene song and story," and participation in a capacity-enhancement grant for the Navajo Language Academy. Publications include "Orality, Literacy, and the Translator: A Case Study in Haida Translation" (forthcoming), for the journal *Translation Studies*, and "Animal Grammar: Wolverine's Soundscape," in the Alaska Native Language Center's *Dene Languages Conference Proceedings 2016* (2017).

CHRISTINE STEWART works in the English and Film Studies Department at the University of Alberta on Treaty 6 territory and unceded Papaschase land. She teaches and studies innovative poetics in the creative writing program. She is a founding member of the Writing Revolution in Place Creative Research Collective and is co-developing a class called "Treaty Six Poetics" with nêhiyaw language instructor and knowledge keeper Reuben Quinn. Recent publications include "Propositions from Under Mill Creek Bridge," in *Sustaining the West* (Wilfrid Laurier University Press); "On Treaty Six from Under Mill Creek Bridge," in *Toward. Some. Air* (Banff Centre Press); and *The Odes,* a chapbook from Nomados Press (shortlisted for the

bpNichol Chapbook award, 2016). A new poetic study of Treaty 6 is forthcoming from Talonbooks.

LISA SZABO-JONES's family emigrated to Canada from the UK in the late
1960s and settled by the ocean, on the traditional territory of the Semiahmoo
Nation. Lisa came to photography in her early teens. Academia led her away
from and back to photography, to co-founding and co-editing *The Goose: A
Journal of Arts, Environment, and Culture in Canada,* to writing and publishing
creative and critical works about ecology and cultural responses to environmental issues. Lisa's photographic technique merges historic processes with digital
ones. Her current (and ongoing) coastal projects combine these visual practices
with research storytelling. She teaches literature at a CÉGEP near Montreal.

DR. ZOE TODD (Métis/otipemisiw) is from amiskwaciwâskahikan (Edmonton), Alberta, Canada. She writes about fish, art, Métis legal traditions, Métis futurisms, the Anthropocene, extinction, and decolonization
in urban and prairie contexts. She has also studied human–animal relations,
colonialism, and environmental change in north/western Canada.

RITA WONG lives and works on unceded Coast Salish Territories, also known
as Vancouver, BC, Canada. Dedicated to questions of water justice, decolonization, and ecology, she is the author of *monkeypuzzle, forage, sybil unres*t
(with Larissa Lai), *undercurrent,* and *perpetual* (with Cindy Mochizuki), as
well as the co-editor of *Downstream: Reimagining Water* (with Dorothy Christian). Wong is a poet-scholar who teaches at the Emily Carr University of Art
and Design.

Index

academic research: colonial ways of knowing as barrier to storytelling, xi, 174–75, 177; need for education reform, xiii; research storytelling, xii–xiii; storytelling for negotiating, 162, 163–65, 167–68, 169–70, 172–73, 178–79. *See also* Métis methodology

Activating the Heart (workshop), xii, xiv, 36–37

"The Adventures of Beaulieu" (Mandeville), 130–31, 132

aesthetic, 35

Agamben, Giorgio, 31, 32, 51n2

áístomatoo'p (Blackfoot cosmology), 41

allies, 21–22

anthropology, 161, 162–63, 165, 169. *See also* Métis methodology

Armstrong, Jeanette, 91

ArtDays: introduction, xv–xvi, 94; background, 94; creative mediums used in, 100; cultural safety, 104–5; future endeavours, 116–17; insights by medical students, 106, 108–10; insights by Nak'azdli participants, 105–6, 107–8; intended spirit of interactions, 100–102; Kendra's background, 92; methodology of sessions, 102–3; Nak'azdli First Nation's Kwah Community Hall location, 95–96; northern British Columbia context, 93–94; participants, 99; purpose, 94, 98–99, 115–16; role of art in Indigenous interactions with medicine, 111–12; Sarah's background, 92–93; storytelling approach, 91–92, 94–95, 115, 174; UBC's Northern Medical Program and, 96–98; values and principles, 103; youth T-shirt workshop, 113, 114, 115

arts-based practices. *See* ArtDays

arts-based research, xii. *See also* research storytelling

Attawapiskat First Nation, 40

Auer, Peter, 65

avant-garde poetics, 52n15

Battiste, Marie, xiii

bilingual narratives. *See* Kaska narrative performances, and code-switching

Blackfoot. *See* Niitsitapi (Blackfoot) people

Bringhurst, Robert, 120, 121, 124, 140n3

British Columbia: Provincial Health Officer's 2007 Annual Report, 112

British Columbia, northern: First Nations Health Authority, 93; ideas and assumptions about, 8–9, 92, 93; Indigenous peoples in, 93–94; as remote, 104–5; UBC Faculty of Medicine's Northern Medical Program, 96–98. *See also* ArtDays; Burns Lake (BC), community-based action research

Burns Lake (BC), community-based action research: introduction, xv, 3–4; author's introduction to colonialism, 12–14, 15; author's introduction to reconciliation, 16–17; author's starting point, 4, 6–8; beginning of project, 12; Burns Lake overview, 9–11; Burns Lake stereotypes and concerns, 8–9; colonialism overview, 4–6; divisions between Native and non-Native, 14–15; filmmaking and dialogue process, 18–19; goal of project, 12; lessons about reconciliation, 20–22; personal lessons for author, 22–24; reconciliation prerequisites, 6; reconciliation results, 19–20; returning home from, 25; use of storytelling, 173–74, 175–76, 177

"The Cannibal" (Mandeville), 130, 140n4, 142n15
Cardinal, Bob, 45, 47
Cardinal, Lewis, 51n8
caribou, 127–29, 130–31, 132. *See also* Mandeville, François, story cycle
Chandler, Michael, 113
Charon, Rita, 115
Chenopodium urbicum (upright goosefoot), 51n5
Cheslatta Carrier people, 16
Christianity, 46, 88n5

Clifford, James, 169
code-switching. *See* Kaska narrative performances, and code-switching
colonialism, 4–6, 13–14, 15, 16, 39–40, 92. *See also* reconciliation
community-based work. *See* Burns Lake (BC), community-based action research
Coney (Yellowknife) River, 145
confrontation, 163–64
creative research making, xii. *See also* research storytelling
Cree. *See* nêhiyaw (Cree) people
cultural safety (cultural humility), 94, 99, 104–5, 108–9

Dancygier, Barbara, 125
Dane-zaa (Beaver) people: mythic understanding of moose and salt licks, 129, 138, 142n14
de Leeuw, Sarah, 92–93, 96. *See also* ArtDays
Deleuze, Gilles, 137
Delgamuukw v. British Columbia [1997], 41
Dene people: code-switching by, 60–61; hunting practices, 138; narratives in world view of, 141n10; on number four, 128. *See also* Mandeville, François, story cycle
Dene Tha people, 53
Derrida, Jacques, 137
diamond mining, 145
Dick, Maudie, 54–55, 57–58, 68
Dickson, John, 55, 56–57, 61, 72, 88n5
Donald, Dwayne, 37, 38, 43, 44, 45, 47, 165–66. *See also* Indigenous Métissage
"Dzǫhdié' Kills the Giant Worm (First Act)" (Kaska story), 68–71

Edmonton (AB). *See* Underbridge Project (Edmonton, AB)

"Education" (Mandeville), 126
education reform, xiii
Elk Woman story, 43–44, 46–47
environmental issues, xvi, 145
Episkenew, Jo-Ann, xvii, 171, 175, 177
Evans, Mike, 166

Feld, Steven, 50
Ferguson, Max, xvi, 152. *See also* Old
   Rawhide (radio personality),
   memories of
Ferrara, Nadia, 112
First Nations: considerations for working with, 117n2; definition, 117n1. *See
   also* colonialism; Indigenous peoples;
   reconciliation
First Nations Health Authority (FNHA),
   93
flesh, 121. *See also* Mandeville, François,
   story cycle
Forcier, Baptiste, 129, 130
Foucault, Michel, 137
frame metonymy, 123–26, 135. *See also*
   Mandeville, François, story cycle
freedom, 47

Garneau, David, 163–64, 166, 170
gender: Kaska code-switching and, 55,
   56–58; in Kaska language, 87n4
"The Girl Who Lived with Salmon"
   (Kaska story), 55, 72–87
Goulet, Jean-Guy, 141n10
Guattari, Félix, 137
Gumperz, John, 58
Gurstein, Penny, 25

Health Arts Research Centre (HARC),
   94, 96, 116. *See also* ArtDays
Heavy Head, Ryan, 41, 43
Heggert, Paul, 35
Highway 16 (Highway of Tears), 9

"His Grandmother Raised Him"
   (Mandeville), 128, 129, 130, 131, 132
"How Copper Was Discovered" (Man-
   deville), 127–28, 131, 132, 138, 139n2
"How Iron Was Discovered" (Mande-
   ville), 128
hunting: Dene practices, 138
Hymes, Dell, 161

Indian Act, 5–6, 16
Indigenous Métissage, 153, 160, 165–66,
   169, 170
Indigenous peoples: in anthropology,
   165; First Nations Health Authority,
   93; in northern British Columbia,
   93–94; reconnection with homelands, 161–62; research focused on,
   104. *See also* Cheslatta Carrier people;
   colonialism; Dane-zaa (Beaver)
   people; Dene people; First Nations;
   nêhiyaw (Cree) people; Niitsitapi
   (Blackfoot) people; reconciliation
intellectual property rights, 168
interpreters, xiv
inter-semiotic translation, 122, 139
The Invisible Committee, 42, 47

Jackson, Michael, 161
Jacobson, Roman, 122, 139

Kaska narrative performances, and
   code-switching: introduction, xv,
   53, 176; for audience participation,
   66; author's background, 53; for
   changes in voice, 62–64; for dramatic
   emphasis, 61–62; "Dzǫhdīé' Kills
   the Giant Worm (First Act)," 68–71;
   gendered nature of, 55, 56–58; "The
   Girl Who Lived with Salmon," 72–87;
   importance of, 66–67; John Dickson,
   55, 56–57, 61, 72, 88n5; Maudie Dick,

54–55, 57–58, *68*; for meta-pragmatic commentary, 64–65; recording storytellers, 53–55; sophistication of code-switching, 60–61; for sound imitation, 64; strategies for code-switching, 59; transcription notes, 87n1; types of code-switching, 58–59; as undervalued, 66; use of Kaska expressions, 59–60

Kaska people: Christianity and, 88n5; gender in Kaska language, 87n4; language use and support, 55; traditional territory, 54

Kennedy, Dawnis, 177–78

Kiitokiiaapii (Blackfoot Elder), 43–44

King, Thomas, 91

knowledge sharing, xi, xiv, 171, 178

Kolson, Bren, 123. *See also* Old Rawhide (radio personality), memories of

Kulick, Don, 56

LaBelle, Brandon, 35–36, 44, 49

Lalonde, Chris, 113

language, xiv

Leggatt, Jacquie, 30, 34, 36, 37, 38, 48–49. *See also* Underbridge Project (Edmonton, AB)

Li Fang-Kuei, xvi, 119. *See also* Mandeville, François, story cycle

listening: against colonial amnesia, 39–40; effects of listening on the listener, 35–36, 47–48; exclusive listening, 50; inclusive listening, 51; in nêhiyaw (Cree) culture, 41; as practice, 30, 33, 38–39, 50. *See also* Underbridge Project (Edmonton, AB)

loving attachment, 3–4, 23, 24

Lukes, Steven, 167

Mandeville, François, story cycle: approach and introduction, xvi,

119–23, 126–27, 176; alliances and networks, 134–35; on animality, 130; animal types in, 141n11; biography of Mandeville, 119; caribou and aggressive migration, 130; caribou and community development, 128–29, 130; caribou and technological innovation, 128; caribou appearances, 127–29, 130–31, 132; caribou as guides, 127–28; cognitive outlook reflected in, 140n3; cross-linguistic echoes, 141n8; cyclical view of lived experience, 138–39; development of survival skills, 132; extraction of animal parts, 129–30; flesh motif, 121, 127; frame metonymy approach to animal references, 121–22, 123–27, *126, 134, 137*; human dependence on animality, 133; interpretation of story cycle as a whole, 142n12; intersection of human and caribou trails, 130–31; inter-semiotic translation in, 122, 139; as intertextual, 136–38; literary style, 120; mobility of narratives, 120–21, 139n2; moose appearances, 131, 132–33; question of contiguity/contingency vs. analogy, 124–25, 135–36; relational ontology, 131; wolf appearances, 131–34

Mandeville, François, specific stories: "The Adventures of Beaulieu," 130–31, 132; "The Cannibal," 130, 140n4, 142n15; "Education," 126; "His Grandmother Raised Him," 128, 129, 130, 131, 132; "How Copper Was Discovered," 127–28, 131, 132, 138, 139n2; "How Iron Was Discovered," 128; "The Man Who Became a Wolf," 121–22, 127, 131–34, 138, 139n1; "Old Axe—Story One," 130, 132; "Old Axe—Story Two," 130, 132; "Raven Head," 128–29, 132, 142n13; "Scabby," 140n5

"The Man Who Became a Wolf"
(Mandeville), 121–22, 127, 131–34, 138, 139n1
Marcel, Fred, 129
mark making, 100
McAdam, Sylvia (Saysewahum), 42–43, 44–45, 47
McNiff, Shaun, xiii
medicine: narrative medicine, 113; role of art in Indigenous interactions with, 111–12; UBC Faculty of Medicine's Northern Medical Program, 96–98; ways of knowing in, 110–11. See also ArtDays
Medicine, Beatrice, 165
Menard, Andrea, 91
Mercier, Ann, 55
Merleau-Ponty, Maurice, 121, 127, 136
Métis, 161–62
Métis methodology: context for writing about, 160; equal responsibility and benefits, 166–67; Indigenous Métissage approach, 165–66; need for, 166; reciprocity, 166, 168, 169; relational aspect of research, 168–69; scholarship on, 165; storytelling, 167–68, 169–70, 172–73. See also Todd, Zoe
metonymy, frame, 123–26, 135. See also Mandeville, François, story cycle
Mill Creek Ravine, 51nn7–9. See also Underbridge Project (Edmonton, AB)
Mitchell-Foster, Kendra, 92. See also ArtDays
miyo-wahkohtôwin (Cree natural law concept of interrelations), 44–46
Moore, Patrick, 123. See also Kaska narrative performances, and code-switching
moose, 129, 131, 132–33, 142n14. See also Mandeville, François, story cycle

Moure, Erín, 35
Musqueam Indian Band, 25
Myers-Scotton, Carol, 59, 60

Nagy, Murielle, 168
Nak'azdli First Nation, 94, 95–96, 99. See also ArtDays
narrative medicine, 113
narrative research, xii. See also research storytelling
narratives. See stories and storytelling
nêhiyaw (Cree) people: on hum in universe, 42–43; interpersonal relationships, 112; on listening, 41; miyo-wahkohtôwin (natural law concept of interrelations), 44–46; on treaties, 45–46; in Underbridge Project, 30, 37
Niitsitapi (Blackfoot) people: áístomatoo'p (cosmology), 41; Elk Woman story, 43–44, 46–47
noise, 34, 35–36. See also Underbridge Project (Edmonton, AB)
non-Indigenous. See settlers
northern British Columbia. See British Columbia, northern

"Old Axe—Story One" (Mandeville), 130, 132
"Old Axe—Story Two" (Mandeville), 130, 132
Old Rawhide (radio personality), memories of: introduction, xvi, 152; death of Old Rawhide, 150–51; mother's household role, 147–48; Old Rawhide's radio shows, 149–50; return of Old Rawhide, 151–52; Saturday night activities, 148–49; use of storytelling in, 175
Oliveros, Pauline, 50, 51
oral history, 41

Panther, Klaus-Uwe, 123, 124, 126, 131, 135

Patrick, Lyanna, 25

Paulatuuq (NT), 160, 164, 165, 166. See also Todd, Zoe

power, 167

Rancière, Jacques, 122

"Raven Head" (Mandeville), 128–29, 132, 142n13

reciprocity, 45–46, 166, 168, 169, 177

reconciliation, 3, 6, 16–17, 19–20, 21–22. See also ArtDays; Burns Lake (BC), community-based action research; Underbridge Project (Edmonton, AB)

Regan, Paulette, 25

Reid, Bill, 92

remoteness, 104–5

research storytelling, xii–xiii. See also stories and storytelling

reserves, 5

residential schools, 5, 15

revolution, 42, 46

Ridington, Robin, 129

Royal Commission on Aboriginal Peoples, 111

salt licks, 129, 142n14

Sandercock, Leonie. See Burns Lake (BC), community-based action research

saskatoons, 155, 159–60, 172

Saysewahum (Sylvia McAdam), 42–43, 44–45, 47

"Scabby" (Mandeville), 140n5

Schafer, R. Murray, 34, 49

Scollon, Ronald, 120, 140n3

Scollon, Suzanne, 120, 140n3

settlers: assumptions about and role in northern British Columbia, 8–9, 92, 93; listening against colonialism

of, 39–40; position of, 37; ways of knowing, 91–92, 110–11. See also colonialism; reconciliation

Sherzer, Joel, 141n8

Silko, Leslie, 91

Simpson, Audra, 163, 165

Simpson, George, 158

smallpox, 157–58

Smith, Linda Tuhiwai, 168

sound, vs. noise, 34. See also Underbridge Project (Edmonton, AB)

Spencer, Jasmine. See Mandeville, François, story cycle

Spenser, Edmund, 32

Sterriah, Grady, 54

Stewart, Christine. See Underbridge Project (Edmonton, AB)

Stewart, Haeden, 42, 47

stories and storytelling: approach to, xiv–xv, 171–72; activating the heart through, 177–78; anthropology on, 161; barriers to in academy, xi, 174–75, 177; in Dene world view, 141n10; interconnections from, xiv, xvi–xvii; for knowledge sharing, 171; as methodology, 94–95, 161, 172–74; narrative medicine, 113; for negotiating scholarship, 162, 163–65, 167–68, 169–70, 172–73, 178–79; as political and epistemological act, 171, 175–77; research storytelling, xii–xiii; significance of, 91, 115; in youth suicide prevention, 113

suicide prevention, in youth, 113

swan down, 88n6

therapeutic planning intervention, 3

Tidd, Claude, 56, 57

Todd, William Ernest, 156, 157–58

Todd, Zoe: introduction, xvi, 153; in Aberdeen (Scotland), 156,

158–59; childhood memories, 154–55; context to memoir and theoretical reflections, 160; experience in anthropology as Métis, 162–63; at family's "homeland," 157; reflections on ancestors, 156–58; saskatoons in Aberdeen, 159–60; storytelling in scholarship, 162, 163–65, 167–68, 169–70, 172–73, 175. *See also* Métis methodology

translation: vs. interpretation, xiv; intersemiotic translation, 122, 139

treaties, 44–45, 45–46

Truth and Reconciliation Commission of Canada, 178

Uexküll, Jakob von, 30, 31–33, 39, 51n2

Umwelt, 31–33

Underbridge Project (Edmonton, AB): introduction, xv, 30, 176–77; author's position, 31, 33; beginning of project, 30–31; compositional notes on recordings, 48–49; effects of listening on the listener, 35–36, 47–48; Elk Woman story on ecological interrelations, 43–44, 46–47; freedom in interrelations, 47; history of Mill Creek Ravine, 51nn8–9; homeless Indigenous people living under Mill Creek Bridge, 30–31, 40; inability to escape interrelations, 46–47; lessons from underbridge spaces, 37–38; listening against colonial amnesia, 39–40; listening as practice, 30, 33, 38–39, 50; listening exercises, 50–51; listening in nêhiyaw (Cree) culture, 41; materiality of relationships, 41–42; miyo-wahkohtôwin (Cree

natural law concept of interrelations), 44–46; noise from under Mill Creek Bridge, 34–35; non-Indigenous position, 37; "Notes from the Underbridge" playlist, 38, 49; obligation to listen to land and inhabitants, 36–37; original name of Mill Creek Ravine, 51n7; political and social implications, 42–43; Schafer's acoustic sensibility, 34; treaties, 45–46; Uexküll's *Umwelt* concept of environment, 31–33

University of British Columbia: Faculty of Medicine's Northern Medical Program, 96–98; School of Community and Regional Planning, 25. *See also* ArtDays

upright goosefoot (*Chenopodium urbicum*), 51n5

Urrutia, Anselmo, 141n8

Venne, Sharon, 41, 47

Voegelin, Salomé, 35, 44

Westerkamp, Hildegard, 49

Wiens, Jeanette, 60

Wilson, Shawn, 169

Winthrop-Young, Geoffrey, 32

wolves, 131–34. *See also* Mandeville, François, story cycle

Wong, Rita: "sleepless in Somba K'e," xvi, 145, 175–76

World Soundscape Project, 34

Yellowknife (Coney) River, 145

youth: suicide prevention, 113; T-shirt workshop, 113, *114*, 115

Žižek, Slavoj, 46, 47, 52n15

BOOKS IN THE INDIGENOUS STUDIES SERIES
PUBLISHED BY WILFRID LAURIER UNIVERSITY PRESS

Blockades and Resistance: Studies in Actions of Peace and the Temagami Blockades of 1988–89 / Bruce W. Hodgins, Ute Lischke, and David T. McNab, editors / 2003 / xi + 276 pp. / illus. / ISBN 0-88920-381-4

Indian Country: Essays on Contemporary Native Culture / Gail Guthrie Valaskakis / 2005 / x + 293 pp. / illus. / ISBN 0-88920-479-9

Walking a Tightrope: Aboriginal People and Their Representations / Ute Lischke and David T. McNab, editors / 2005 / xix + 377 pp. / illus. / ISBN 978-0-88920-484-3

The Long Journey of a Forgotten People: Métis Identities and Family Histories / Ute Lischke and David T. McNab, editors / 2007 / viii + 386 pp. / illus. / ISBN 978-0-88920-523-9

Words of the Huron / John L. Steckley / 2007 / xvii + 259 pp. / ISBN 978-0-88920-516-1

Essential Song: Three Decades of Northern Cree Music / Lynn Whidden / 2007 / xvi + 176 pp. / illus., musical examples, audio CD / ISBN 978-0-88920-459-1

From the Iron House: Imprisonment in First Nations Writing / Deena Rymhs / 2008 / ix + 147 pp. / ISBN 978-1-55458-021-7

Lines Drawn upon the Water: First Nations and the Great Lakes Borders and Borderlands / Karl S. Hele, editor / 2008 / xxiii + 351 pp. / illus. / ISBN 978-1-55458-004-0

Troubling Tricksters: Revisioning Critical Conversations / Linda M. Morra and Deanna Reder, editors / 2009 / xii+ 336 pp. / illus. / ISBN 978-1-55458-181-8

Aboriginal Peoples in Canadian Cities: Transformations and Continuities / Heather A. Howard and Craig Proulx, editors / 2011 / viii + 256 pp. / illus. / ISBN 978-1-055458-260-0

Bridging Two Peoples: Chief Peter E. Jones, 1843–1909 / Allan Sherwin / 2012 / xxiv + 246 pp. / illus. / ISBN 978-1-55458-633-2

The Nature of Empires and the Empires of Nature: Indigenous Peoples and the Great Lakes Environment / Karl S. Hele, editor / 2013 / xxii + 350 / illus. / ISBN 978-1-55458-328-7

The Eighteenth-Century Wyandot: A Clan-Based Study / John L. Steckley / 2014 / x + 306 pp. / ISBN 978-1-55458-956-2

Indigenous Poetics in Canada / Neal McLeod, editor / 2014 / xii + 404 pp. / ISBN 978-1-55458-982-1

Literary Land Claims: The "Indian Land Question" from Pontiac's War to Attawapiskat / Margery Fee / 2015 / x + 318 pp. / illus. / ISBN 978-1-77112-119-4

Arts of Engagement: Taking Aesthetic Action in and beyond Canada's Truth and Reconciliation Commission / Dylan Robinson and Keavy Martin, editors / 2016 / viii + 376 pp. / illus. / ISBN 978-1-77112-169-9

Learn, Teach, Challenge: Approaching Indigenous Literature / Deanna Reder and Linda M. Morra, editors / 2016 / xii + 580 pp. / ISBN 978-1-77112-185-9

Read, Listen, Tell: Indigenous Stories from Turtle Island / Sophie McCall, Deanna Reder, David Gaertner, and Gabrielle L'Hirondelle Hill, editors / 2017 / xviii + 390 pp. / ISBN 978-1-77112-300-6

Violence Against Indigenous Women: Literature, Activism, Resistance / Allison Hargreaves / 2017 / xvi + 281 pp. / ISBN 978-1-77112-239-9

Activating the Heart: Storytelling, Knowledge Sharing, and Relationship / Julia Christensen, Christopher Cox, and Lisa Szabo-Jones, editors / 2018 / xviii + 212 pp. / ISBN 978-1-77112-219-1